Wee Wonder Quilts

Some occasions just demand hand-made gifts. Celebrating the birth of a new baby is right there at the top of my list. When I see a baby shower invitation in my future, I really want to be ready with something special. Since I also procrastinate, *those* occasions demand a *quick* hand-made gift. Luckily, we have five great patterns right here that even I could have ready in time for the "oohs" and "aahs" from the shower crowd. Take these patterns and add your touch with great fabrics to make the perfect quilt for that bouncing baby boy…or girl…or delightful surprise. If you're like me, you're already running out of time. Go ahead and get started, but before you wrap it all up and give it away, snap a picture of that future heirloom and send it to me at QuiltEditor@leisurearts.com.

Cheryl

Cheryl Johnson
Quilt Publication Director

LEISURE ARTS, INC.
Little Rock, AR

bunny Hop

Finished Quilt Size:
45" x 45" (114 cm x 114 cm)

YARDAGE REQUIREMENTS

Yardage is based on 43"/44" (109 cm/112 cm) wide fabric with a "usable width" of 40" (102 cm).

- 3/4 yd (69 cm) of blue print fabric
- 3/4 yd (69 cm) of white print fabric
- 1/8 yd (11 cm) **each** of 10-12 assorted pastel print fabrics
- 1/2 yd (46 cm) of bunny print fabric
- 3/8 yd (34 cm) of pink print fabric
- 3/8 yd (34 cm) of brown print fabric for appliqués
- 3 yds (2.7 m) of fabric for backing
- 3/8 yd (34 cm) of fabric for binding

You will also need:

- 53" x 53" (135 cm x 135 cm) piece of batting
- Paper-backed fusible web
- Stabilizer
- Dark blue embroidery floss

CUTTING OUT THE PIECES

Follow ***Rotary Cutting****, page 32, to cut fabric. All strips are cut across the width of the fabric. All measurements include 1/4" seam allowances.*

From blue print fabric:

- Cut 1 strip 10 7/8" wide. From this strip, cut 2 squares 10 7/8" x 10 7/8". Cut each square **once** diagonally for a total of 4 triangles (**A**). Cut the remaining fabric into 2 squares 4 7/8" x 4 7/8". Cut each square **once** diagonally for a total of 4 triangles (**B**).
- Cut 3 strips 4 1/2" wide. From these strips, cut 12 rectangles (**C**) 4 1/2" x 8 1/2".

From white print fabric:

- Cut 1 strip 10 7/8" wide. From this strip, cut 2 squares 10 7/8" x 10 7/8". Cut each square **once** diagonally for a total of 4 triangles (**D**).
- Cut 3 strips 4 1/2" wide. From these strips, cut 24 squares (**E**) 4 1/2" x 4 1/2".

From assorted pastel print fabrics:

- Cut approximately 80-90 strips in varying widths of 1", 1 1/4", 1 1/2" and 1 3/4" by at least 10" in length (**F**).

From bunny print fabric:

- Cut 2 strips 4 1/2" wide. From these strips, cut 4 squares (**G**) 4 1/2" x 4 1/2" and 4 rectangles (**H**) 4 1/2" x 8 1/2".
- Cut 1 square (**I**) 6 1/4" x 6 1/4".

From pink print fabric:

- Cut 2 strips 4 1/2" wide. From these strips, cut 8 rectangles (**J**) 4 1/2" x 6 1/2" and 4 squares (**K**) 4 1/2" x 4 1/2".

From binding fabric:

- Cut 5 strips 2 1/8" wide.

CUTTING OUT THE APPLIQUÉS

Refer to ***Preparing Fusible Appliqués****, page 34, to make appliqués using patterns, page 7. Patterns are reversed and do not include seam allowances.*

From brown print fabric:

- Cut 4 heads.
- Cut 4 ears; cut 4 ears in reverse.

MAKING THE BLOCKS

Follow **Machine Piecing**, *page 33, and* **Pressing**, *page 34. Referring to photo for placement, follow* **Satin Stitch Appliqué**, *page 34, to add appliqués.*

Block A

1. Sew assorted strips (**F**) together to make 4 panels at least 10" x 15"; press seam allowances to 1 side. Trim each panel to 8½" x 14½" to make **Block A**. Set remaining assorted strips aside.

Block A (make 4)

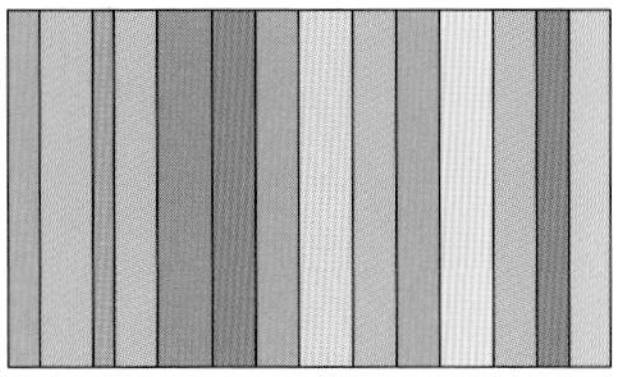

Block B

1. Appliqué bunny pieces to triangle (**D**) to make **Unit 1**. Make 4 Unit 1's.

Unit 1 (make 4)

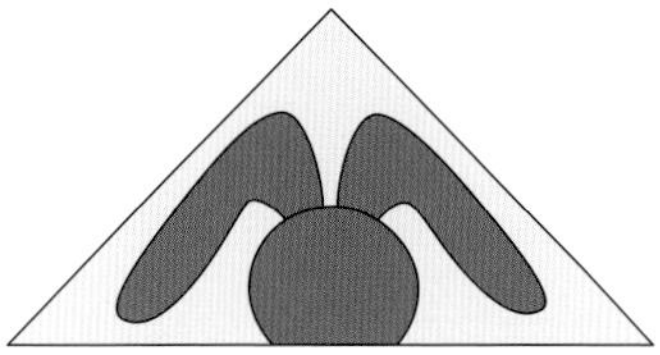

2. Sew 1 **Unit 1** to 1 triangle (**A**) to make **Unit 2**. Make 4 Unit 2's.

Unit 2 (make 4)

3. Sew 1 square (**G**) to 1 rectangle (**J**) to make **Unit 3**. Make 4 Unit 3's.

Unit 3 (make 4)

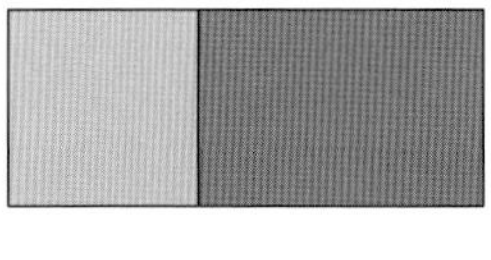

4. Sew 1 **Unit 3** to 1 **Unit 2** to make **Unit 4**. Make 4 Unit 4's.

Unit 4 (make 4)

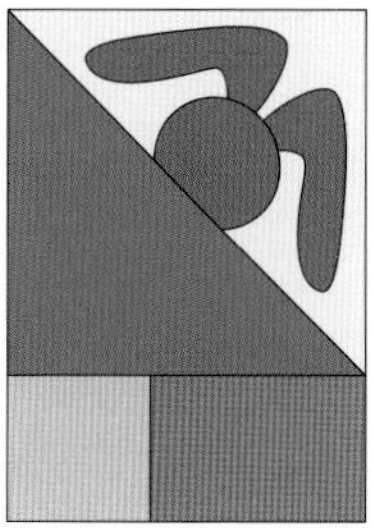

5. Sew 1 rectangle (**H**) to 1 rectangle (**J**) to make **Unit 5**. Make 4 Unit 5's.

Unit 5 (make 4)

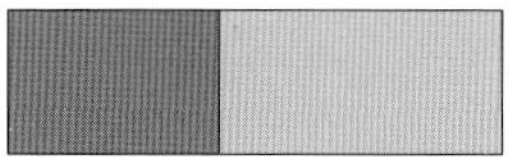

6. Sew 1 **Unit 5** to 1 **Unit 4** to make **Block B**. Make 4 Block B's.

Block B (make 4)

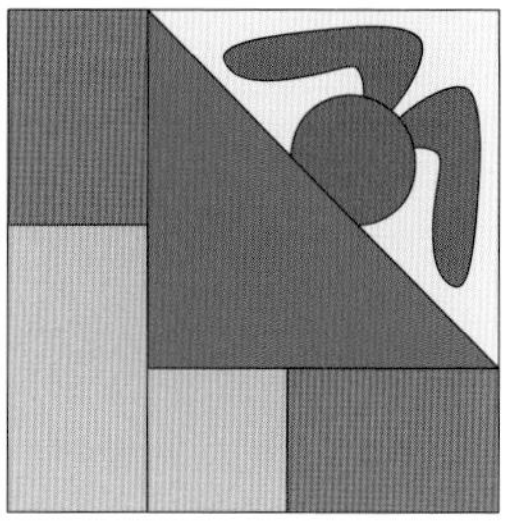

7. Use 2 strands of floss and an Outline Stitch to embroider bunnies' noses and mouths. Use 2 strands of floss and a Satin Stitch to embroider bunnies' eyes to complete **Block B's**.

Block C

1. Sew 1 triangle (**B**) to opposite sides of 1 square (**I**) to make **Unit 6**.

Unit 6

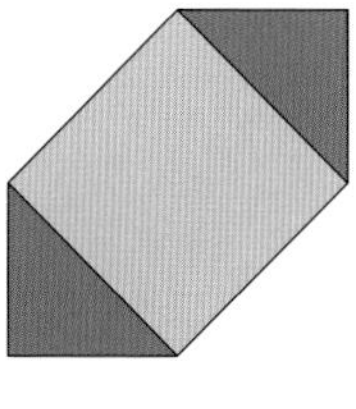

2. Sew 1 triangle (**B**) to remaining sides of **Unit 6** to make **Block C**.

Block C

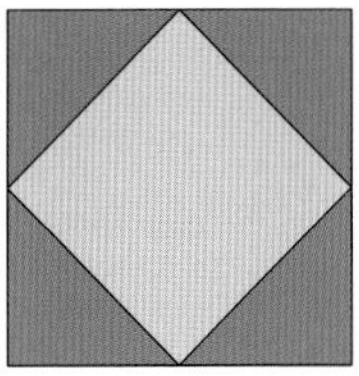

ASSEMBLING THE QUILT TOP CENTER

*Refer to **Quilt Top Diagram**, page 7, to assemble quilt top.*

1. Sew 2 **Block B's** and 1 **Block A** together to make **Row A**. Make 2 Row A's.

Row A (make 2)

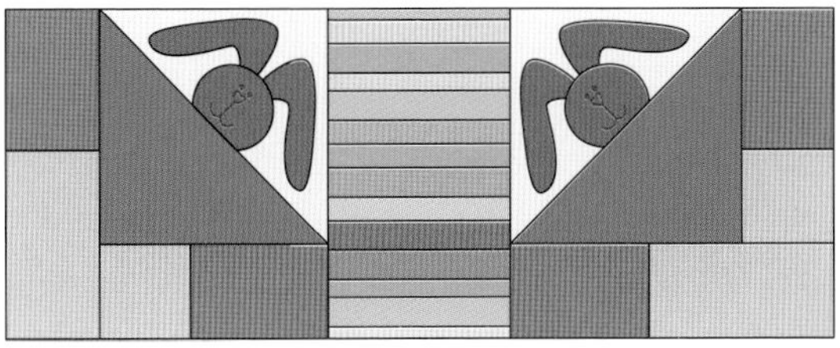

2. Sew 2 **Block A's** and 1 **Block C** together to make **Row B**.

Row B

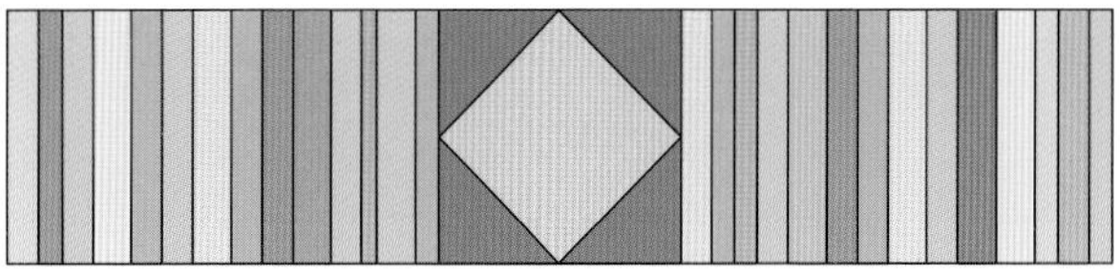

3. Sew **Rows** together to make **Quilt Top Center**.

ADDING THE BORDERS

1. Sew assorted strips (**F**) together to make 1 panel at least 10" x 28"; press seam allowances to one side. From this panel, cut 8 **Border Strips** 4½" x 6½" as shown in **Fig. 1**.

Fig. 1

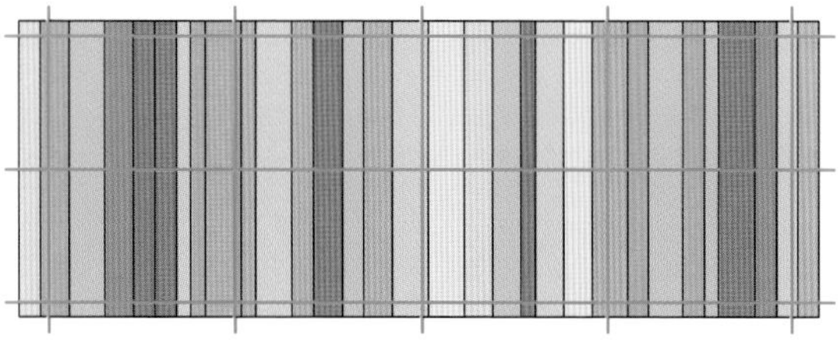

Border Strips (make 8)

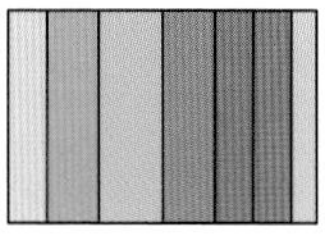

2. Draw a diagonal line (corner to corner) on wrong side of squares (**E**).
3. Place 1 marked square (**E**) on 1 end of rectangle (**C**) and stitch diagonally (**Fig. 2**). Trim ¼" from stitching line (**Fig. 3**). Open up and press, pressing seam allowances toward darker fabric (**Fig. 4**).

Fig. 2

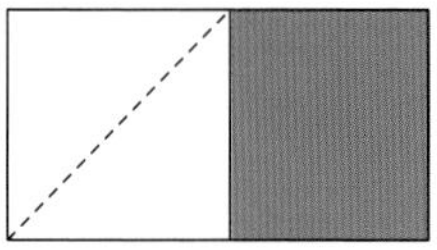

Fig. 3

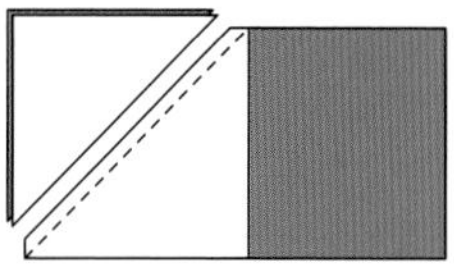

Fig. 4

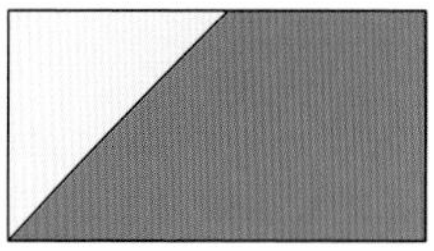

4. Place another marked square (**E**) on opposite end of rectangle. Stitch and trim as shown in **Fig. 5**. Open up and press to complete **Flying Geese Unit**. Make 12 Flying Geese Units.

Fig. 5

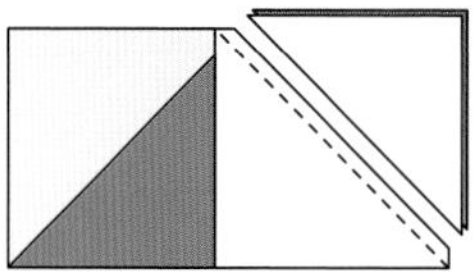

Flying Geese Unit (make 12)

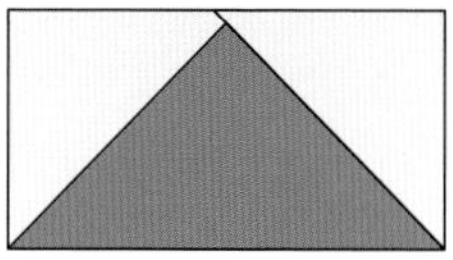

5. Sew 3 **Flying Geese Units** and 2 **Border Strips** together to make **Border**. Make 4 Borders.

Border (make 4)

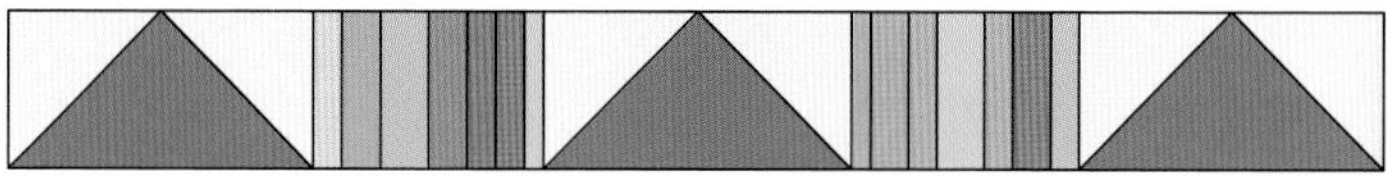

6. Matching centers and corners, sew 1 **Border** to opposite sides of Quilt Top Center.
7. Sew 1 square (**K**) to each end of 2 Borders to make **Top/Bottom Borders**.
8. Matching centers and corners, sew **Top/Bottom Borders** to Quilt Top Center to complete **Quilt Top**.

COMPLETING THE QUILT

1. Follow **Quilting**, page 35, to mark, layer, and quilt as desired. Our quilt was machine quilted with an all-over meandering stitch.
2. Refer to **Making a Hanging Sleeve**, page 38, to make and attach a hanging sleeve, if desired.
3. Follow **Binding**, page 39, to bind quilt using binding strips.

Quilt Top Diagram

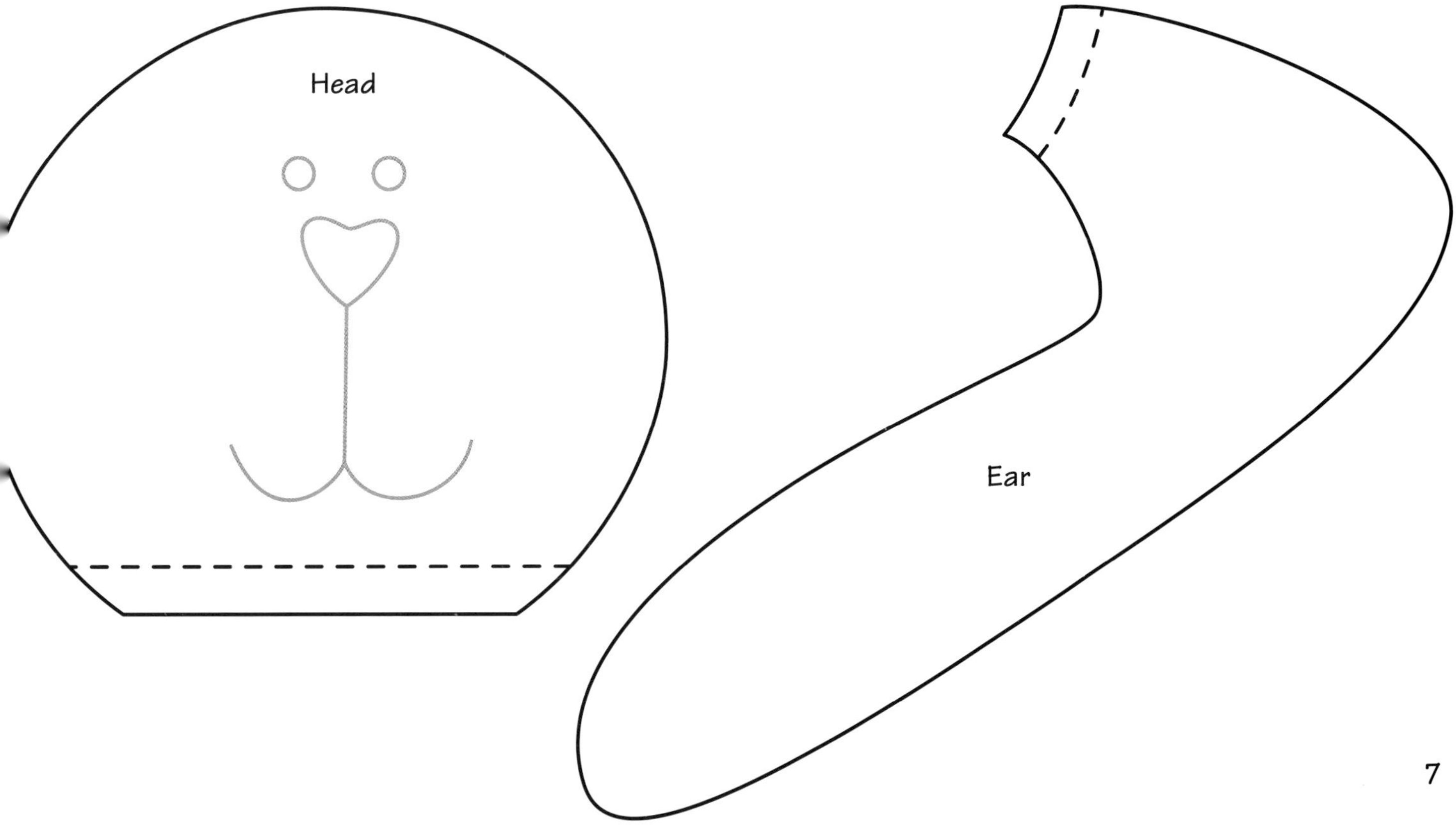

duck, duck, Goose...

Finished Quilt Size:
53" x 53" (135 cm x 135 cm)
Finished Block Size:
12" x 12" (30 cm x 30 cm)

YARDAGE REQUIREMENTS

Yardage is based on 43"/44" (109 cm/112 cm) wide fabric with a "usable width" of 40" (102 cm).

- 1/4 yd (23 cm) **each** of 9 to 11 assorted pastel print fabrics
- 3/8 yd (34 cm) of lavender print fabric for sashing squares
- 5/8 yd (57 cm) **each** of light yellow print and light blue print fabric for sashings
- 5/8 yd (57 cm) of yellow print fabric for block backgrounds
- 3/4 yd (69 cm) of dark blue print fabric
- 1/4 yd (23 cm) of dark yellow print fabric for appliqués
- 1/4 yd (23 cm) of gold print fabric for appliqués
- 3 1/2 yds (3.2 m) of fabric for backing
- 1/2 yd (46 cm) of fabric for binding

You will also need:

- 61" x 61" (155 cm x 155 cm) piece of batting
- Paper-backed fusible web
- Dark blue embroidery floss

CUTTING OUT THE PIECES

Follow ***Rotary Cutting****, page 32, to cut fabric. All strips are cut across the width of the fabric. All measurements include 1/4" seam allowances.*

From assorted pastel print fabrics:

- Cut 36 large squares (**A**) 4 1/2" x 4 1/2".

From lavender print fabric:

- Cut 2 strips 4 1/2" wide. From these strips, cut 16 squares (**B**) 4 1/2" x 4 1/2".

From light yellow print fabric:

- Cut 8 strips (**C**) 2 1/2" wide.

From light blue print fabric:

- Cut 8 strips (**D**) 2 1/2" wide.

From yellow print fabric:

- Cut 7 strips 2 1/2" wide. From these strips, cut 108 small squares (**E**) 2 1/2" x 2 1/2".

From dark blue print fabric:

- Cut 5 strips 4 1/2" wide. From these strips, cut 72 rectangles (**F**) 2 1/2" x 4 1/2".

From binding fabric:

- Cut 6 binding strips 2 1/8" wide.

CUTTING OUT THE APPLIQUÉS

Refer to ***Preparing Fusible Appliqués****, page 34, to make appliqués using patterns, page 13. Patterns are reversed and do not include seam allowances.*

From dark yellow print fabric:

- Cut 2 duck bodies.
- Cut 1 goose body.

From gold print fabric:

- Cut 2 duck beaks.
- Cut 2 duck wings.
- Cut 2 duck left feet.
- Cut 2 duck right feet.
- Cut 1 goose beak.
- Cut 1 goose wing.
- Cut 1 goose left foot.
- Cut 1 goose right foot.

MAKING THE BLOCKS

1. Sew 4 assorted large squares (**A**) together to make 1 **4-Patch Unit**. Make 9 4-Patch Units.

4-Patch Unit (make 9)

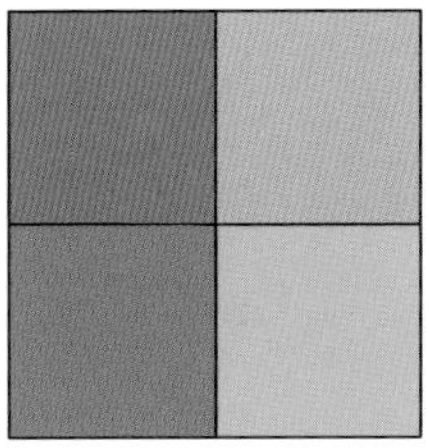

2. Using 72 yellow small squares (**E**), draw a diagonal line on wrong side of fabric from upper left corner to bottom right corner.
3. Matching right sides, lay 1 yellow small square (**E**) on 1 end of 1 rectangle (**F**). Stitch on drawn line (**Fig. 1**). Trim ¼" from stitching line (**Fig. 2**). Press yellow fabric to the upper right to make **Unit 1**. Make 36 Unit 1's.

Fig. 1

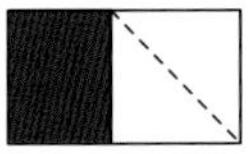

Fig. 2

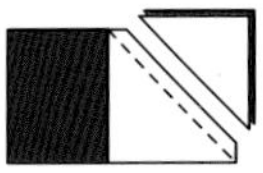

Unit 1 (make 36)

4. Repeat **Step 3** using 36 remaining marked yellow small squares (**E**) and 36 remaining dark blue rectangles (**F**) and placing yellow squares on opposite end of rectangle with drawn line in opposite direction to make a total of 36 **Unit 2's**.

Unit 2 (make 36)

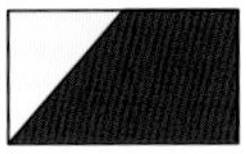

5. Sew 1 Unit 1 and 1 Unit 2 together to make **Unit 3**. Make 36 Unit 3's.

Unit 3 (make 36)

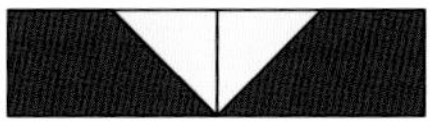

6. Sew 1 Unit 3 to 2 opposite sides of 1 4-Patch Unit to make **Unit 4**. Make 9 Unit 4's.

Unit 4 (make 9)

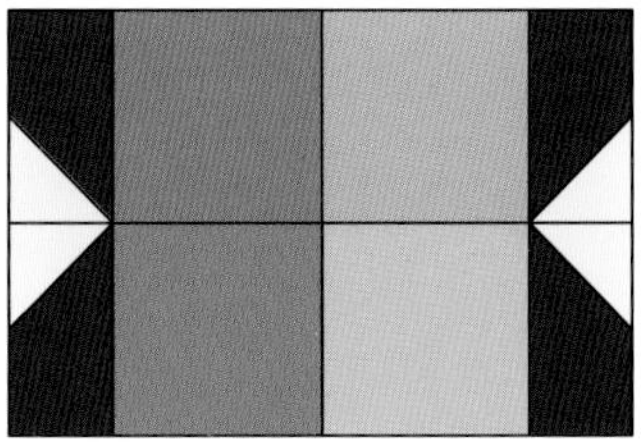

7. Sew 1 square (**E**) to each end of 1 **Unit 3** to make **Unit 5**. Make 18 Unit 5's.

Unit 5 (make 18)

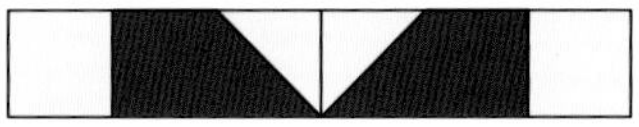

8. Sew 1 Unit 5 to each remaining side of 1 **Unit 4** to make **Block**. Make 9 Blocks.

Block (make 9)

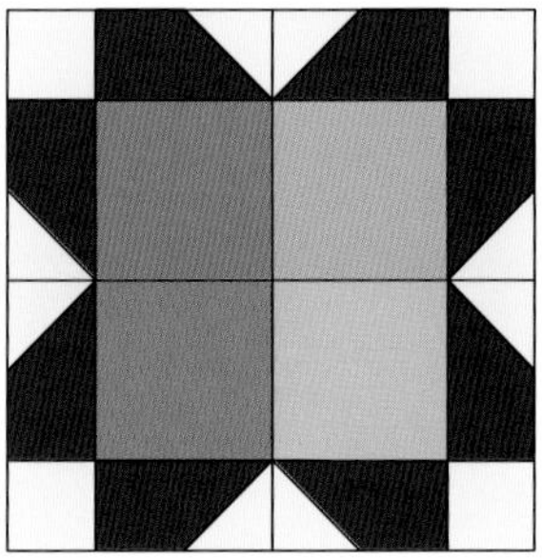

ADDING THE APPLIQUÉS

1. Fuse duck and goose pieces to each of 3 Blocks.
2. Use 2 strands of floss and a Blanket Stitch, page 42, to appliqué duck and goose pieces.
3. Use 2 strands of floss and a French Knot to embroider ducks eyes.

ASSEMBLING THE QUILT TOP

Follow ***Machine Piecing****, page 33, and* ***Pressing****, page 34. Refer to* ***Quilt Top Diagram****, page 12, to assemble quilt top.*

1. Sew 1 strip (**C**) and 1 strip (**D**) together to make **Strip Set**. Make 8 Strip Sets. Cut across Strip Sets at 12½" intervals to make **Unit 6**. Make 24 Unit 6's.

Strip Set (make 8)

Unit 6 (make 24)

2. Sew 4 squares (**B**) and 3 Unit 6's together to make **Sashing Row**. Make 4 Sashing Rows.

Sashing Row (make 4)

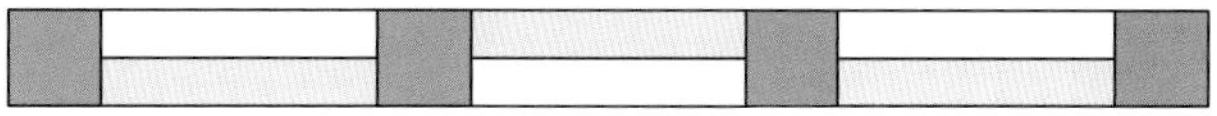

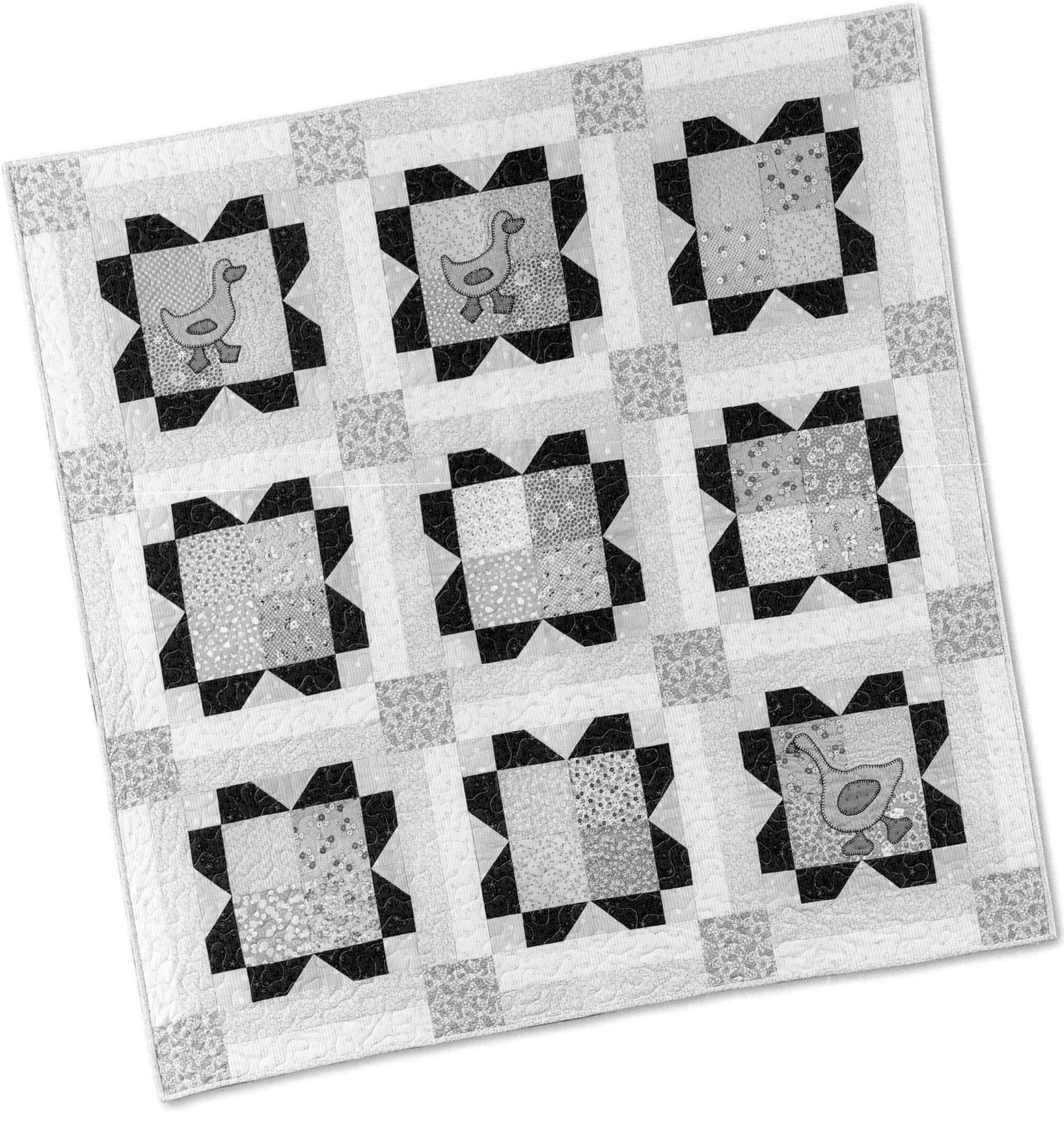

3. Sew 4 Unit 6's and 3 Blocks together to make **Block Row**. Make 3 Block Rows.

Block Row (make 3)

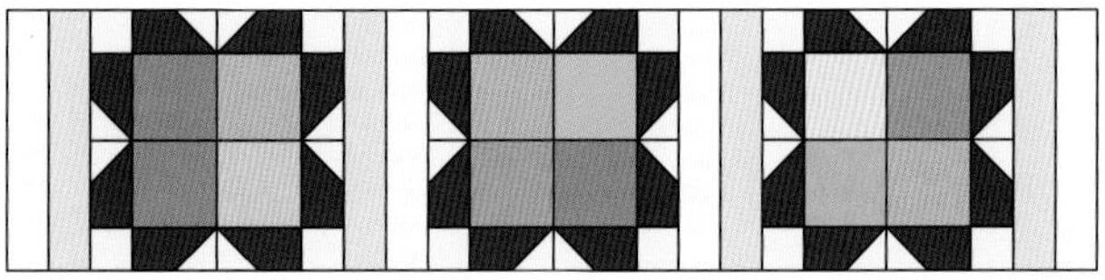

4. Sew Sashing Rows and Block Rows together to complete **Quilt Top**.

COMPLETING THE QUILT

1. Follow **Quilting**, page 35, to mark, layer, and quilt as desired. Our quilt was machine quilted with an all-over meandering stitch.
2. Refer to **Making a Hanging Sleeve**, page 38, to make and attach a hanging sleeve, if desired.
3. Follow **Binding**, page 39, to bind quilt using binding strips.

Quilt Top Diagram

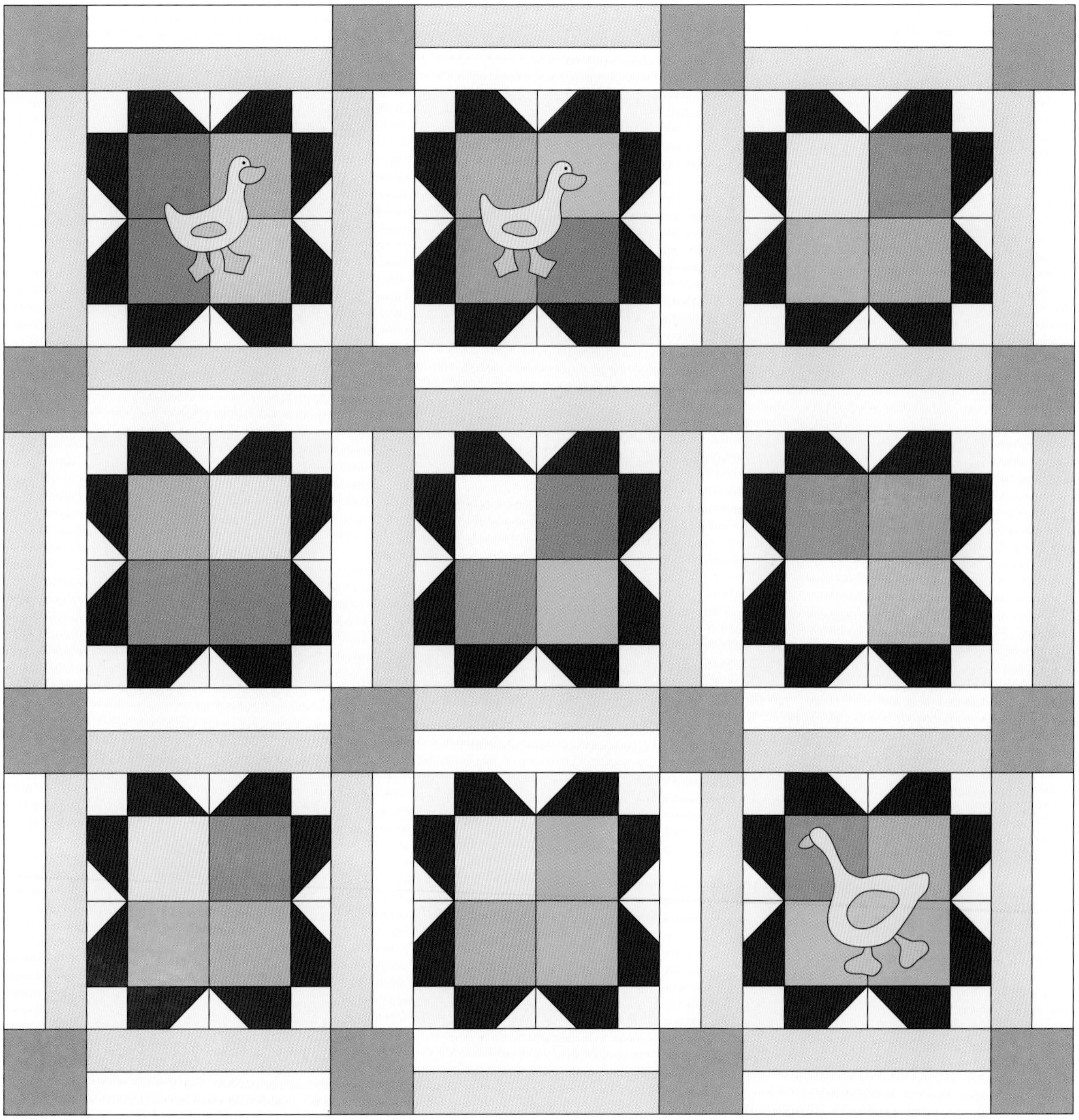

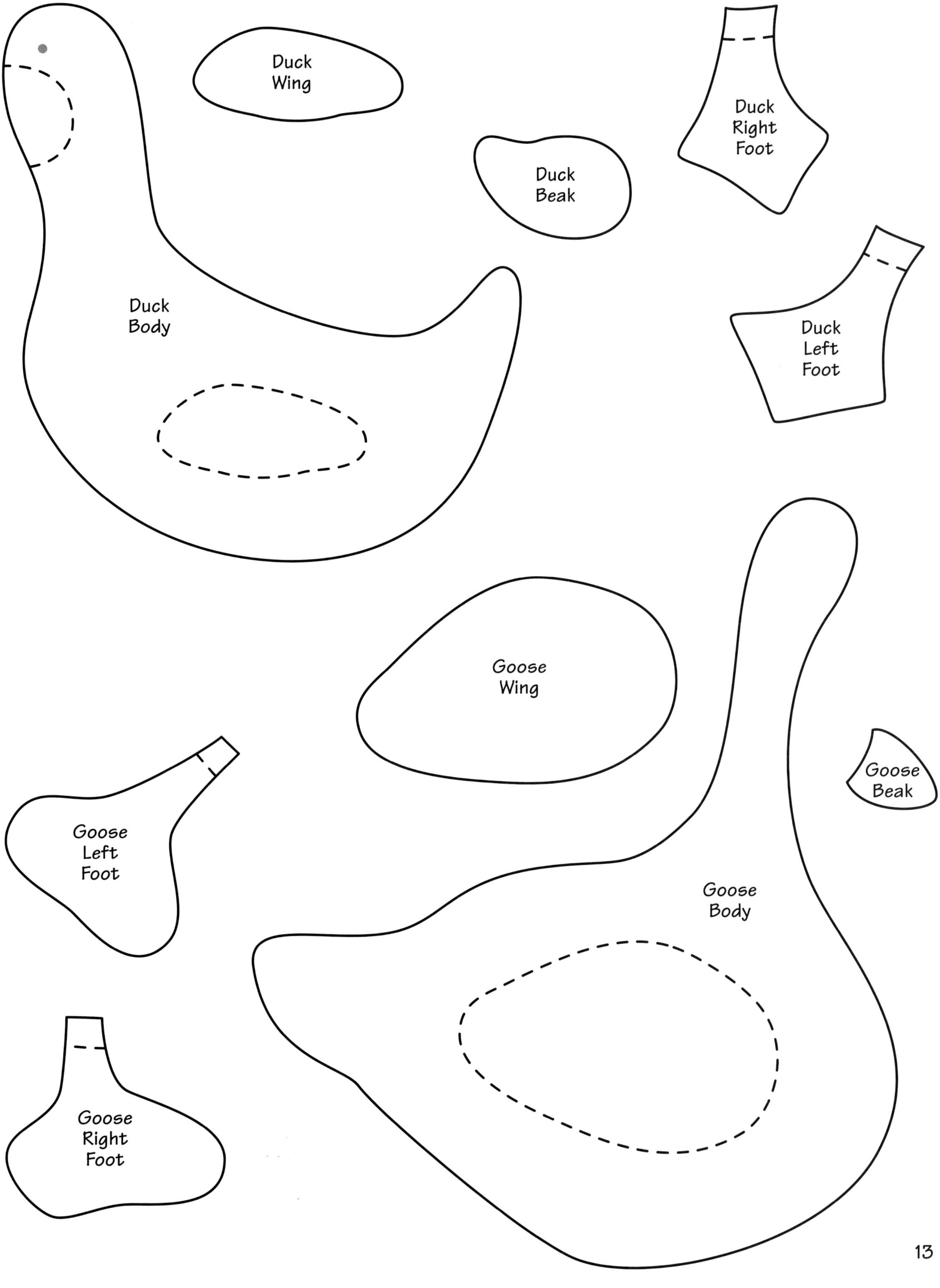
Duck Wing
Duck Right Foot
Duck Beak
Duck Left Foot
Duck Body
Goose Wing
Goose Beak
Goose Left Foot
Goose Body
Goose Right Foot

hearts Aplenty

Finished Quilt Size:
45" x 45" (114 cm x 114 cm)

YARDAGE REQUIREMENTS

Yardage is based on 43"/44" (109 cm/112 cm) wide fabric with a "usable width" of 40" (102 cm).

- 3/8 yd (34 cm) of heart print fabric
- 3/4 yd (69 cm) of yellow print fabric
- 7/8 yd (80 cm) of blue print fabric
- 1/2 yd (46 cm) **total** of assorted bright print fabrics
- 1/4 yd (23 cm) of red print fabric for appliqués
- 3 yds (2.7 m) fabric for backing
- 3/8 yd (34 cm) fabric for binding

You will also need:

- 53" x 53" (135 cm x 135 cm) piece of batting
- Paper-backed fusible web
- Stabilizer

CUTTING OUT THE PIECES

Follow **Rotary Cutting**, *page 32, to cut fabric. All strips are cut across the width of the fabric. All measurements include 1/4" seam allowances.*

From heart print fabric:

- Cut 2 strips 4 1/2" wide. From these strips, cut 8 rectangles (**A**) 4 1/2" x 6 1/2" and 4 squares (**B**) 4 1/2" x 4 1/2".

From yellow print fabric:

- Cut 3 strips 2 1/2" wide (**C**). Cut 1 of these strips in half (**D**).
- Cut 1 strip 2 1/2" wide. From this strip, cut 4 squares (**E**) 2 1/2" x 2 1/2" and 4 rectangles (**F**) 2 1/2" x 4 1/2".
- Cut 3 strips 4 1/2" wide. From these strips, cut 16 rectangles (**G**) 4 1/2" x 6 1/2".

From blue print fabric:

- Cut 3 strips (**H**) 2 1/2" wide. From 1 strip, cut 13 squares (**I**) 2 1/2" x 2 1/2". Cut 1 strip in half (**J**) at fold. Discard 1 half strip.
- Cut 5 border strips (**K**) 3 1/2" wide.

From assorted bright print fabrics:

- Cut 72 squares (**L**) 2 1/2" x 2 1/2"
- From **each** of 4 assorted fabrics, cut 1 rectangle (**M**) 2 1/2" x 4 1/2" and 2 rectangles (**N**) 2 1/2" x 6 1/2".

From binding fabric:

- Cut 5 strips (**O**) 2 1/8" wide.

CUTTING OUT THE APPLIQUÉS

Refer to **Preparing Fusible Appliqués**, *page 34, to make appliqués using heart pattern, page 19. Pattern does not include seam allowances.*

From red print fabric:

- Cut 16 hearts.

MAKING THE BLOCKS

*Follow **Machine Piecing**, page 33, and **Pressing**, page 34. Refer to **Quilt Top Diagram**, page 19, to assemble quilt top. Referring to photo for placement, follow **Satin Stitch Appliqué**, page 34, to add appliqués.*

9-Patch Block

1. Making sure blue print square (**I**) is in the center, sew 1 square (**I**) and 8 squares (**L**) together to make 1 **9-Patch Block**. Make 9 9-Patch Blocks.

9-Patch Block (make 9)

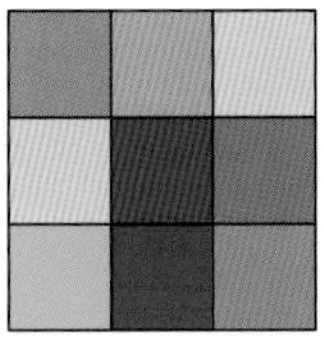

Log Block

1. Sew 1 square (**I**) and 1 square (**E**) together to make **Unit 1**. Make 4 Unit 1's.

Unit 1 (make 4)

2. Sew 1 rectangle (**F**) to 1 **Unit 1** to make **Unit 2**. Make 4 Unit 2's.

Unit 2 (make 4)

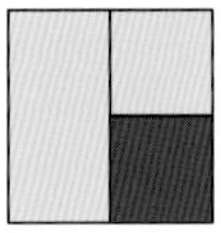

3. Sew 1 rectangle (**M**) to 1 **Unit 2** to make **Unit 3**. Make 4 Unit 3's.

Unit 3 (make 4)

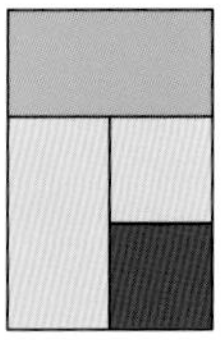

4. Sew 1 rectangle (**N**) to 1 **Unit 3** to make **Log Block**. Make 4 Log Blocks.

Log Block (make 4)

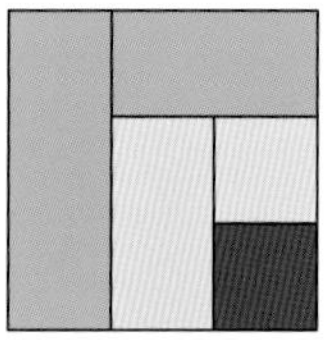

Heart Block

1. Center and appliqué 1 heart to 1 rectangle (**G**) to make **Unit 4**. Make 16 Unit 4's.

Unit 4 (make 16)

2. Sew 1 rectangle (**N**) and 1 **Heart Block** together to make **Heart Block**. Make 4 Heart Blocks.

Heart Block (make 4)

Rail Block

1. Sew 2 strips (**C**) and 1 strip (**H**) together to make **Strip Set A**.

Strip Set A

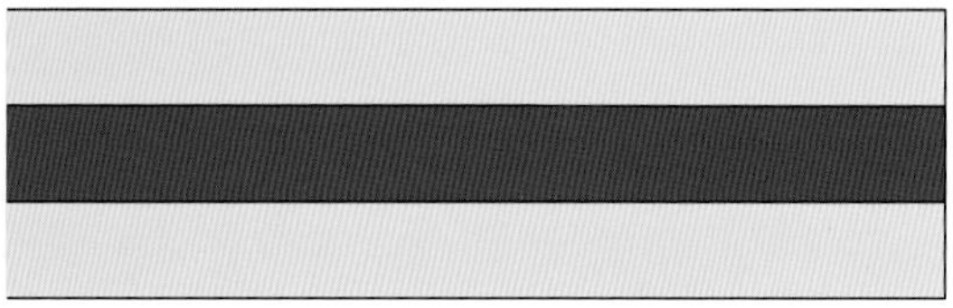

2. Sew 2 strips (**D**) and 1 strip (**J**) together to make **Strip Set B**.

Strip Set B

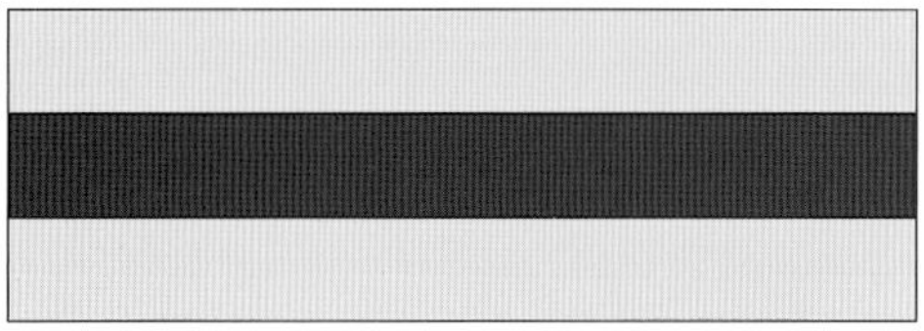

3. Cut across Strip Set A and Strip Set B at $6^{1}/_{2}$" intervals to make **Rail Block**. Make 8 Rail Blocks.

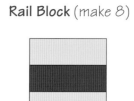

Rail Block (make 8)

ASSEMBLING THE QUILT TOP CENTER

Refer to ***Quilt Top Diagram*** *to assemble quilt top.*

1. Sew 2 squares (**B**), 3 **Unit 4's**, and 2 rectangles (**A**) together to make **Row A**. Make 2 Row A's.

Row A (make 2)

2. Sew 2 **Unit 4's**, 3 **9-Patch Blocks**, and 2 **Rail Blocks** together to make **Row B**. Make 2 Row B's.

Row B (make 2)

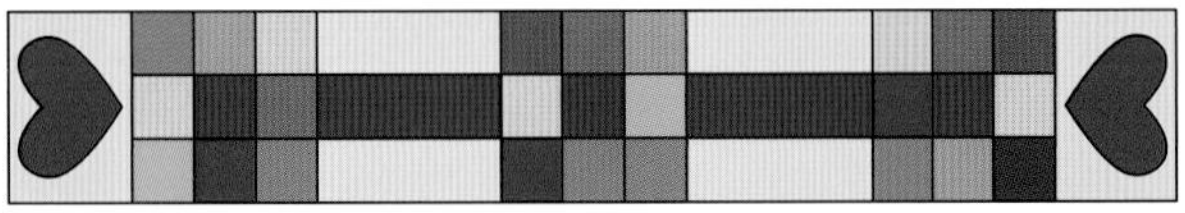

3. Sew 2 rectangles (**A**), 2 **Rail Blocks**, 2 **Log Blocks**, and 1 **Heart Block** together to make **Row C**. Make 2 Row C's.

Row C (make 2)

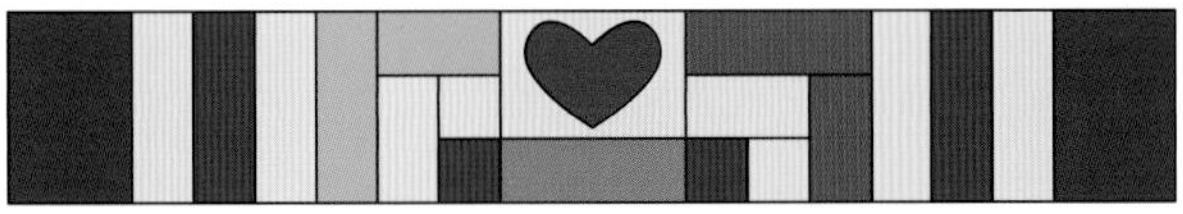

4. Sew 2 **Unit 4's**, 3 **9-Patch Blocks**, and 2 **Heart Blocks** together to make **Row D**.

Row D

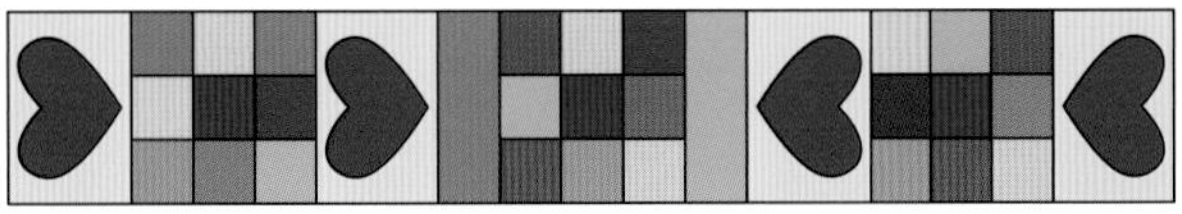

5. Sew **Rows A-D** together to complete **Quilt Top Center**.

ADDING THE BORDERS

1. To determine length of side borders, measure **length** of quilt top center. From border strips (**K**), cut 2 **side borders** the determined length. Matching centers and corners, sew side borders to Quilt Top Center.
2. Sew remaining border strips (**K**) together end to end.
3. To determine length of top/bottom borders, measure **width** of quilt top (including added borders). From pieced border strip, cut 2 **top/bottom borders** the determined length. Matching centers and corners, sew top/bottom borders to quilt top to complete **Quilt Top**.

COMPLETING THE QUILT

1. Follow **Quilting**, page 35, to mark, layer, and quilt as desired. Our quilt was machine quilted with an all-over meandering stitch.
2. Refer to **Making a Hanging Sleeve**, page 38, to make and attach a hanging sleeve, if desired.
3. Follow **Binding**, page 39, to bind quilt using binding strips.

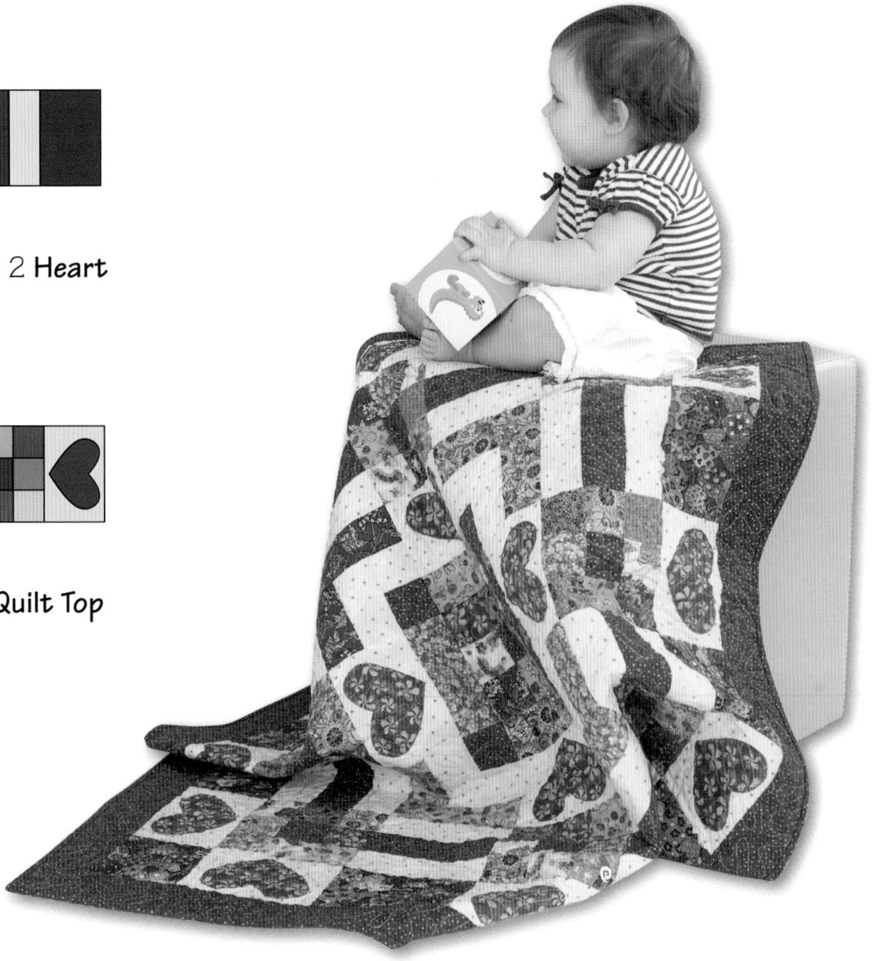

Quilt Top Diagram

hop, skip, Jump...

Finished Quilt Size:
$42^1/_2$" x $42^1/_2$" (108 cm x 108 cm)
Finished Block Size:
$13^1/_2$" x $13^1/_2$" (34 cm x 34 cm)

YARDAGE REQUIREMENTS

Yardage is based on 43"/44" (109 cm/112 cm) wide fabric with a "usable width" of 40" (102 cm).

- $^1/_4$ yd (23 cm) of white print fabric
- $^3/_8$ yd (34 cm) of red check fabric
- $^5/_8$ yd (57 cm) of blue print fabric
- $1^1/_8$ yds (1 m) of yellow print fabric
- $^3/_8$ yd (34 cm) of green print fabric
- $2^7/_8$ yds (2.6 m) of fabric for backing
- $^3/_8$ yd (34 cm) of fabric for binding

You will also need:

- 51" x 51" (130 cm x 130 cm) piece of batting

CUTTING OUT THE PIECES

Follow **Rotary Cutting**, *page 32, to cut fabric. All strips are cut across the width of the fabric. All measurements include $^1/_4$" seam allowances.*

From white print fabric:

- Cut 1 strip (**A**) $3^1/_2$" wide.
- Cut 2 strips (**B**) 2" wide.

From red check fabric:

- Cut 2 strips (**C**) $3^1/_2$" wide. Cut 1 strip in half (**D**) at the fold. Discard 1 half strip.
- Cut 2 strips (**E**) 2" wide.

From blue print fabric:

- Cut 3 strips (**F**) 2" wide. Cut 1 strip in half (**G**) at the fold. From 1 of the half strips, cut 5 squares (**H**) 2" x 2".
- Cut 4 border strips (**I**) $1^1/_2$" wide.
- Cut 1 strip $5^1/_2$" wide. From this strip, cut 4 border squares $5^1/_2$" x $5^1/_2$" (**J**).

From yellow print fabric:

- Cut 1 strip 5" wide. From this strip, cut 8 rectangles (**K**) $3^1/_2$" x 5".
- Cut 1 strip (**L**) 2" wide.
- Cut 2 strips (**M**) $3^1/_2$" wide.
- Cut 8 border strips (**N**) $2^1/_2$" wide.

From green print fabric:

- Cut 6 strips (**O**) 2" wide. Cut 2 of these strips into 4 sashing strips (**P**) 2" x 14".

From binding fabric:

- Cut 5 binding strips (**Q**) $2^1/_8$" wide.

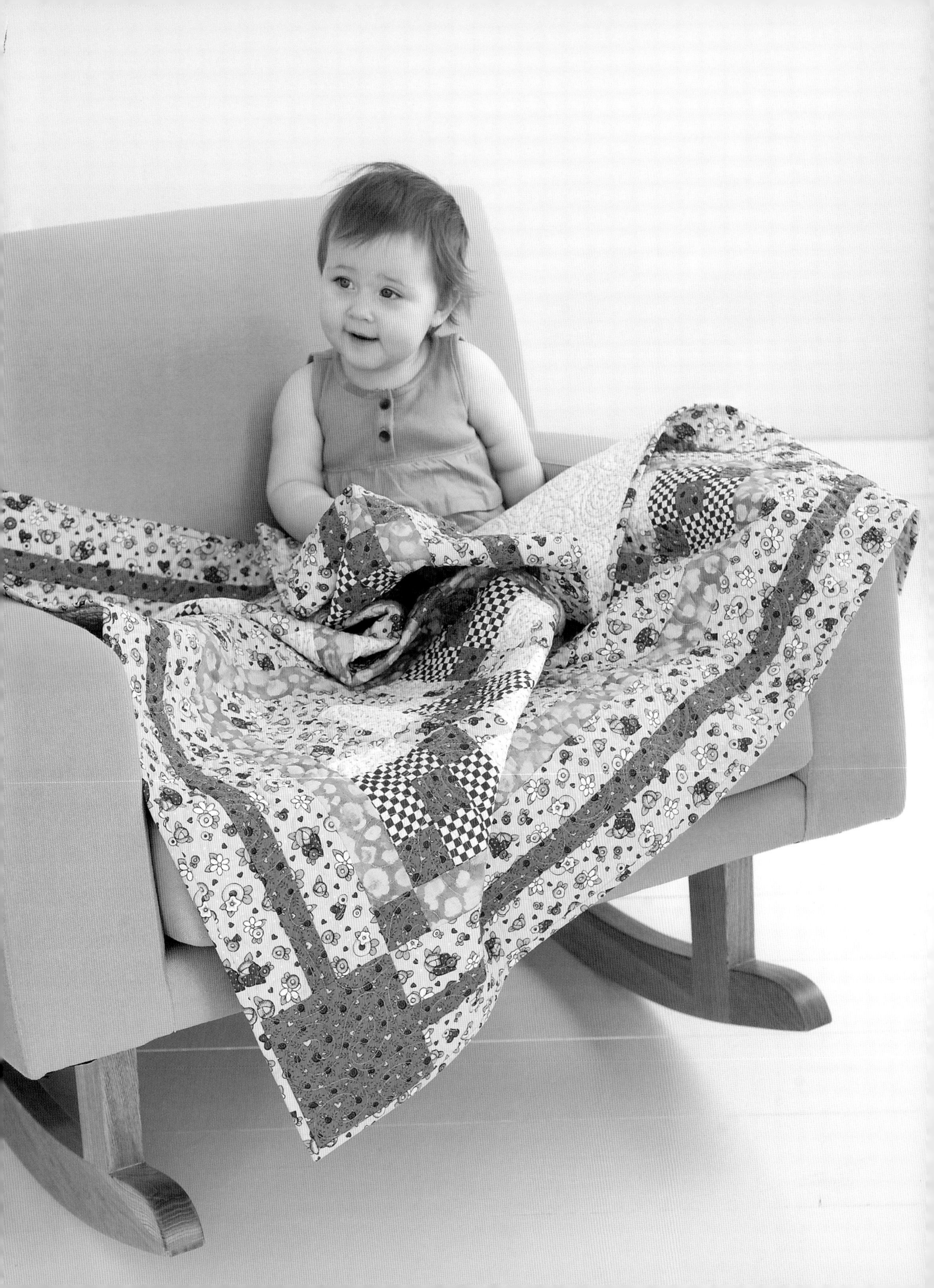

MAKING THE BLOCKS

*Follow **Machine Piecing**, page 33, and **Pressing**, page 34. Match right sides and use a $^1/_4$" seam allowance throughout.*

1. Sew 2 strips (**E**) and 1 strip (**F**) together to make **Strip Set A**. Cut across Strip Set A's at 2" intervals to make **Unit 1**. Make 12 Unit 1's.

Strip Set A

Unit 1 (make 12)

2. Sew 1 strip (**C**) and 1 strip (**F**) together to make **Strip Set B**. Sew 1 half strip (**D**) and 1 half strip (**G**) together to make **Strip Set C**. Cut across Strip Set B's and C's at 2" intervals to make **Unit 2**. Make 24 Unit 2's.

Strip Set B

Strip Set C

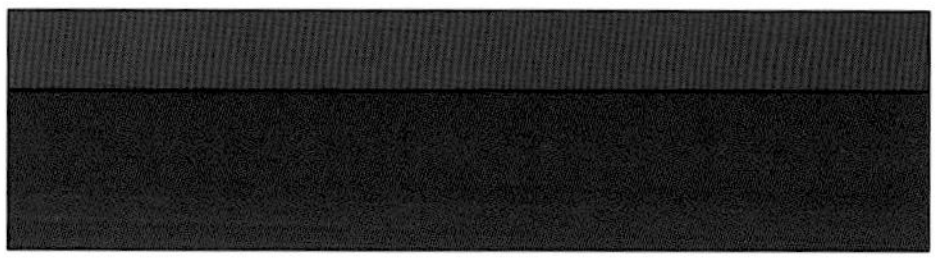

Unit 2 (make 24)

3. Sew 1 strip (**A**) and 1 strip (**L**) together to make **Strip Set D**. Cut across Strip Set D's at 2" intervals to make **Unit 3**. Make 16 Unit 3's.

Strip Set D

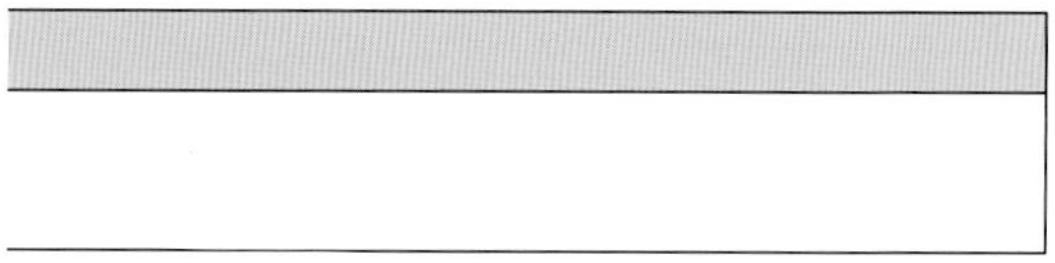

Unit 3 (make 16)

4. Sew 1 strip (**M**) and 1 strip (**B**) together to make **Strip Set E**. Make 2 Strip Set E's. Cut across Strip Set E's at $3^1/_2$" intervals to make **Unit 4's** and at 2" intervals to make **Unit 5**. Make 16 Unit 4's and 8 Unit 5's.

Strip Set E (make 2)

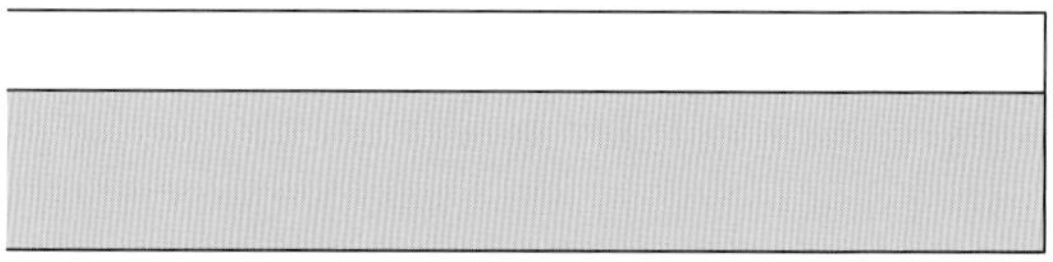

Unit 4 (make 16)

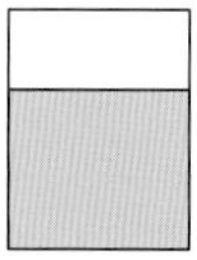

Unit 5 (make 8)

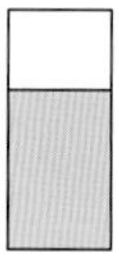

5. Sew 2 Unit 2's and 1 Unit 1 together to make **Unit 6**. Make 12 Unit 6's.

Unit 6 (make 12)

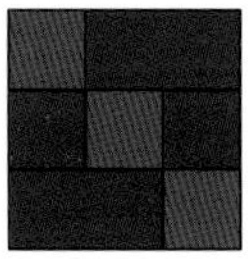

6. Sew 1 Unit 3 and 1 Unit 4 together to make **Unit 7**. Make 16 Unit 7's.

Unit 7 (make 16)

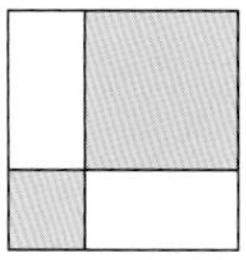

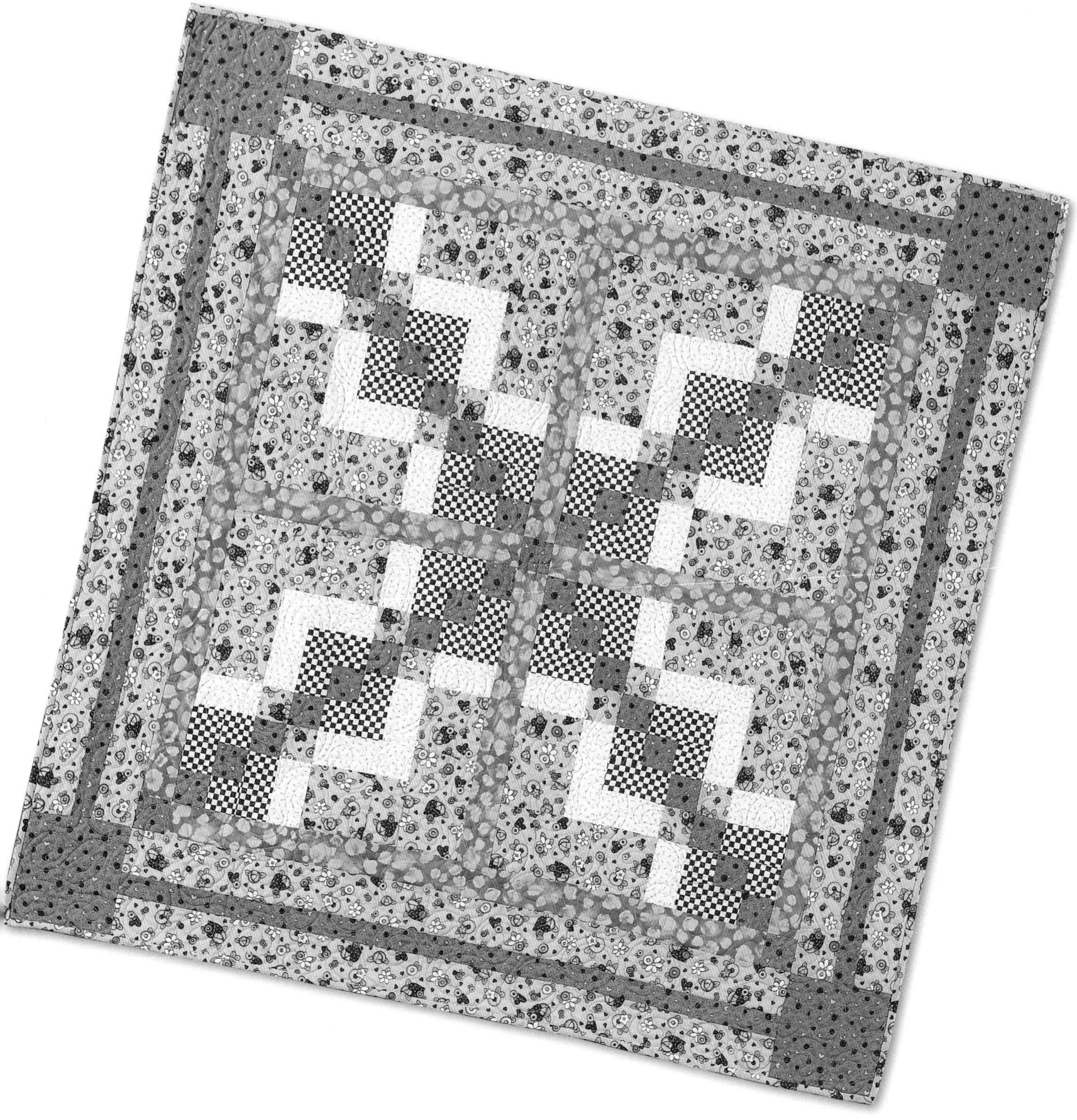

7. Sew 1 Unit 5 and 1 rectangle (**K**) together to make **Unit 8**. Make 8 Unit 8's.

Unit 8 (make 8)

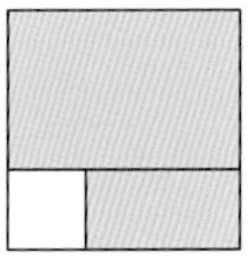

8. Refer to Block Assembly Diagram to sew 3 **Unit 6's**, 4 **Unit 7's**, and 2 **Unit 8's** together to make **Block**. Make 4 Blocks.

Block Assembly Diagram

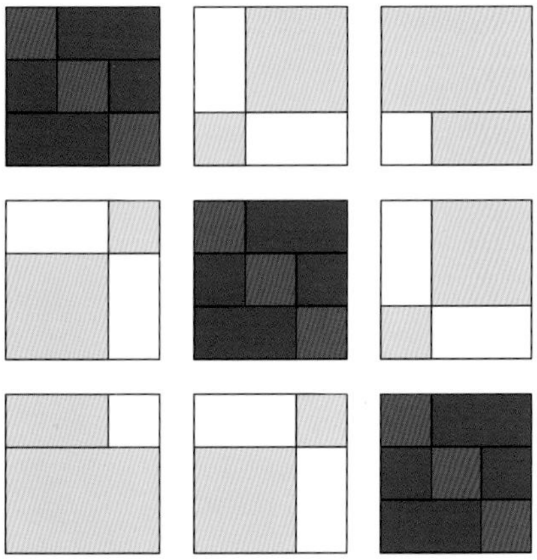

Block (make 4)

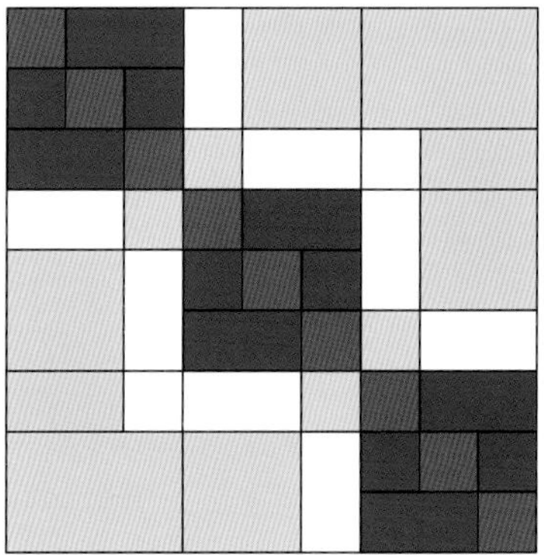

ASSEMBLING THE QUILT TOP CENTER

*Refer to **Quilt Top Diagram** to assemble quilt top.*

1. Sew 2 **Blocks** and 1 sashing strip (**P**) together to make **Row A**. Make 2 Row A's.
2. Sew 2 sashing strips (**P**) and 1 square (**H**) together to make **Row B**.
3. Sew **Row A's** and **Row B** together to make **Quilt Top Center**.

ADDING THE BORDERS

1. Measure **length** of quilt top center. From strips (**O**), cut 2 **inner side borders** the determined length. **Do not** attach at this time.
2. To determine length of inner top/bottom borders, measure **width** of Quilt Top Center. From remaining strips (**O**), cut 2 **inner top/bottom borders** the determined length.
3. Matching centers and corners, sew inner side borders to Quilt Top Center.
4. Sew 1 square (**H**) to each end of inner top and bottom borders.
5. Matching centers and corners, sew inner top/bottom borders to Quilt Top Center.
6. Sew 2 border strips (**N**) and 1 border strip (**I**) together to make **outer border**. Make 4 outer borders.

Outer Border (make 4)

7. To determine length of outer side borders, measure **length** of quilt top. From outer border, cut 2 **outer side borders** the determined length. **Do not** attach at this time.
8. To determine length of outer top/bottom borders, measure **width** of quilt top center. From remaining outer borders, cut 2 **outer top/bottom borders** the determined length.
9. Matching centers and corners, sew outer side borders to Quilt Top.
10. Sew 1 square (**J**) to each end of outer top/bottom borders.
11. Matching centers and corners, sew outer top/bottom borders to quilt top to complete **Quilt Top**.

COMPLETING THE QUILT

1. Follow **Quilting**, page 35, to mark, layer, and quilt as desired. Our quilt was machine quilted with a meandering swirl pattern.
2. Refer to **Making a Hanging Sleeve**, page 38, to make and attach a hanging sleeve, if desired.
3. Follow **Binding**, page 39, to bind quilt using binding strips.

Quilt Top Diagram

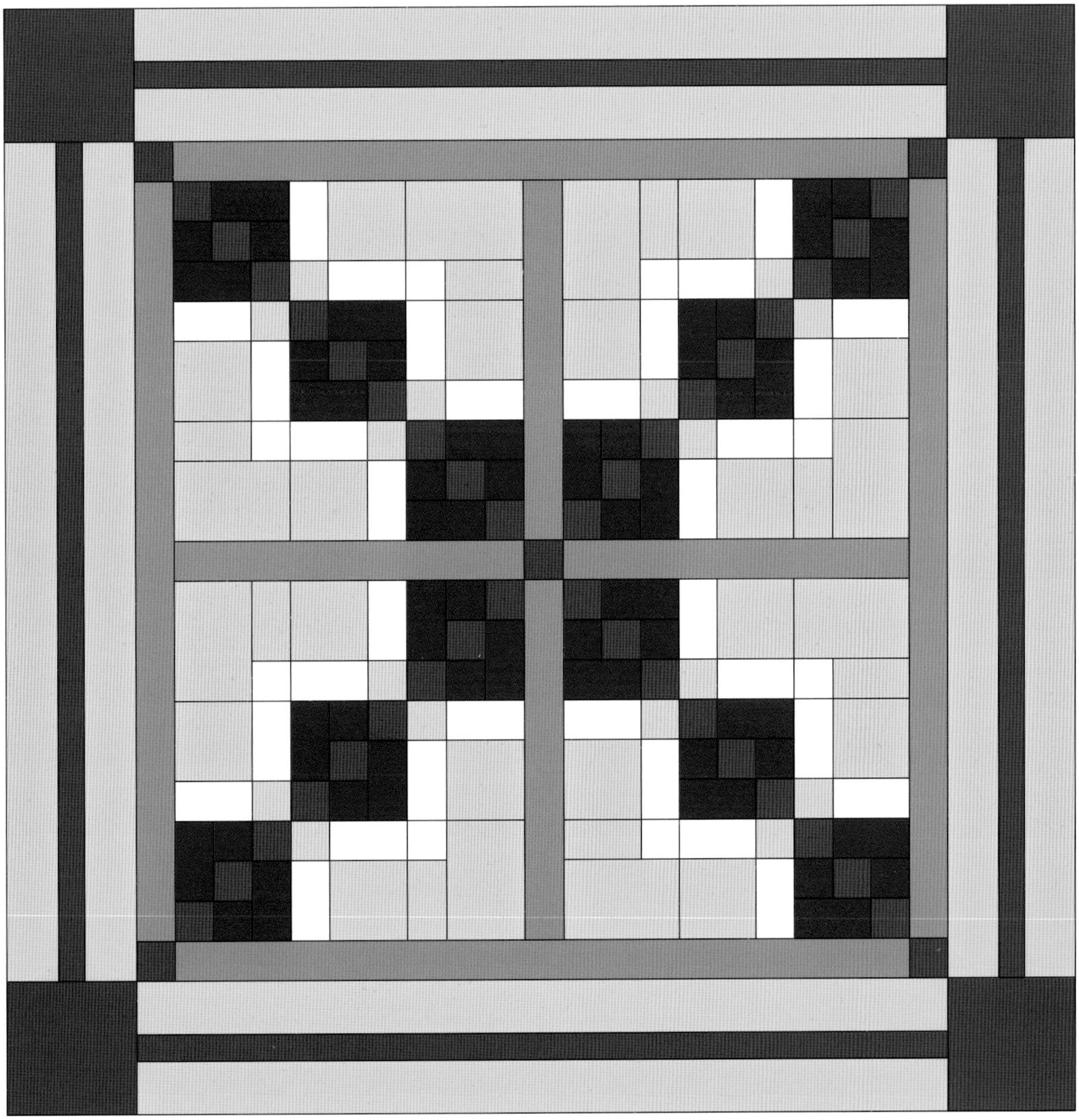

peek-a-Boo

Finished Quilt Size:
$51^1/_2$" x $51^1/_2$" (131 cm x 131 cm)
Finished Block Size:
8" x 8" (20 cm x 20 cm)

YARDAGE REQUIREMENTS

Yardage is based on 43"/44" (109 cm/112 cm) wide fabric with a "usable width" of 40" (102 cm).

- $^1/_4$ yd (23 cm) of novelty print fabric
- $1^1/_2$ yds (1.4 m) of blue print fabric
- $^3/_4$ yd (69 cm) of yellow print fabric
- $^3/_4$ yd (69 cm) of pink print fabric
- $3^3/_8$ yds (3.1 m) of fabric for backing
- $^1/_2$ yd (46 cm) of fabric for binding

You will also need:

- 60" x 60" (152 cm x 152 cm) piece of batting

CUTTING OUT THE PIECES

Follow **Rotary Cutting**, *page 32, to cut fabric. All strips are cut across the width of the fabric. All measurements include $^1/_4$" seam allowances.*

From novelty print fabric:

- Centering design before cutting, "fussy cut" 5 squares (**A**) 4" x 4".

From blue print fabric:

- Cut 1 strip $8^7/_8$" wide. From this strip, cut 4 squares $8^7/_8$" x $8^7/_8$". Cut each square **once** diagonally to make a total of 8 triangles (**B**).
- Cut 2 strips $4^7/_8$" wide. From these strips, cut 16 squares $4^7/_8$" x $4^7/_8$". Cut each square **once** diagonally to make a total of 32 triangles (**C**).
- Cut 1 strip $4^1/_2$" wide. From this strip, cut 4 rectangles (**D**) $4^1/_2$" x $8^1/_2$".
- Cut 5 border strips (**E**) $4^1/_2$" wide.

From yellow print fabric:

- Cut 1 strip $8^7/_8$" wide. From this strip, cut 4 squares $8^7/_8$" x $8^7/_8$". Cut each square **once** diagonally to make a total of 8 triangles (**F**).
- Cut 1 strip $4^1/_2$" wide. From this strip, cut 4 rectangles (**G**) $4^1/_2$" x $8^1/_2$".
- Cut 3 strips $1^1/_2$" wide. From these strips, cut 10 rectangles (**H**) $1^1/_2$" x 4" and 10 rectangles (**I**) $1^1/_2$" x 6".
- Cut 3 strips $1^3/_4$" wide. From these strips, cut 12 rectangles (**J**) $1^3/_4$" x $8^1/_2$"

From pink print fabric:

- Cut 2 strips $4^7/_8$" wide. From these strips, cut 16 squares $4^7/_8$" x $4^7/_8$". Cut each square **once** diagonally to make a total of 32 triangles (**K**).
- Cut 5 strips $1^3/_4$" wide. From these strips, cut 10 rectangles (**L**) $1^3/_4$" x 6" and 10 rectangles (**M**) $1^3/_4$" x $8^1/_2$".
- Cut 2 strips $1^3/_4$" wide. From these strips, cut 8 rectangles (**N**) $1^3/_4$" x $8^1/_2$" and 4 squares (**O**) $1^3/_4$" x $1^3/_4$".

From binding fabric:

- Cut 6 binding strips (**P**) $2^1/_8$" wide.

MAKING THE BLOCKS

*Follow **Machine Piecing**, page 33, and **Pressing**, page 34. Match right sides and use a 1/4" seam allowance throughout.*

Block A

1. Matching long raw edges, sew 1 triangle (**B**) and 1 triangle (**F**) together to make **Block A**. Press seam allowances toward blue fabric. Make 8 Block A's.

Block A (make 8)

Block B

1. Matching long raw edges, sew 1 triangle (**C**) and 1 triangle (**K**) together to make **Unit 1**. Press seam allowances toward blue fabric. Make 32 Unit 1's.

Unit 1 (make 32)

2. Sew 4 Unit 1's together to make **Block B**. Make 8 Block B's.

Block B (make 8)

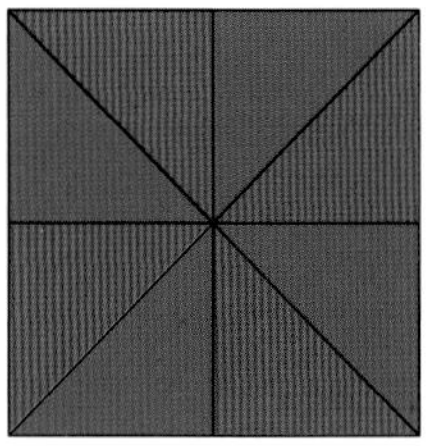

Block C

1. Matching long raw edges, sew 1 rectangle (**D**) and 1 rectangle (**G**) together to make **Block C**. Press seam allowances toward blue fabric. Make 4 Block C's.

Block C (make 4)

Block D

1. Matching raw edges, sew 1 rectangle (**H**) to opposite sides of 1 square (**A**) to make **Unit 2**. Press seam allowances toward yellow fabric. Make 5 Unit 2's.

Unit 2 (make 5)

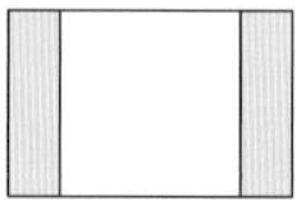

2. Matching raw edges, sew 1 rectangle (**I**) to top and bottom of 1 **Unit 2** to make **Unit 3**. Press seam allowances toward yellow fabric. Make 5 Unit 3's.

Unit 3 (make 5)

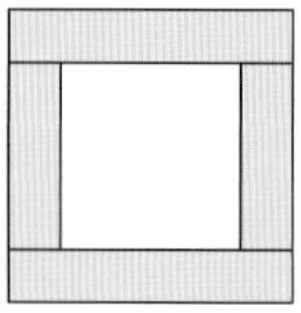

3. Matching raw edges, sew 1 rectangle (**L**) to opposite sides of 1 **Unit 3** to make **Unit 4**. Press seam allowances toward pink fabric. Make 5 Unit 4's.

Unit 4 (make 5)

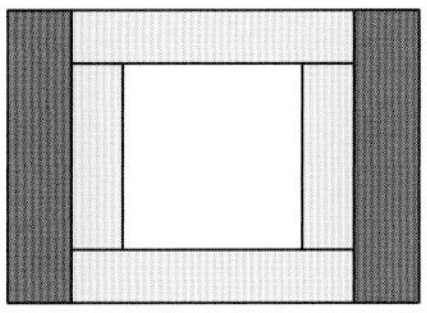

4. Matching raw edges, sew 1 rectangle (**M**) to top and bottom of 1 **Unit 4** to make **Block D**. Press seam allowances toward pink fabric. Make 5 Block D's.

Block D (make 5)

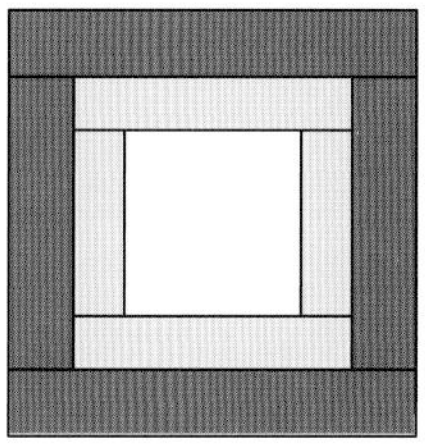

ASSEMBLING THE QUILT TOP CENTER

*Press seam allowances in Rows 1, 3, and 5 in one direction. Press seam allowances in Rows 2 and 4 in opposite direction. Refer to **Quilt Top Diagram** to assemble quilt top.*

1. Sew 3 **Block B's** and 2 **Block A's** together to make **Row A**. Make 2 **Row A's.**
2. Sew 2 **Block A's**, 2 **Block D's**, and 1 **Block C** together to make **Row B**. Make 2 **Row B's.**
3. Sew 2 **Block B's**, 2 **Block C's**, and 1 **Block D** together to make **Row C**.
4. Sew Rows together to make **Quilt Top Center**.

ADDING THE BORDERS

Inner Border

1. Sew 3 rectangles (**J**) and 2 rectangles (**N**) together to make **Inner Border**. Make 4 Inner Borders.

Inner Border (make 4)

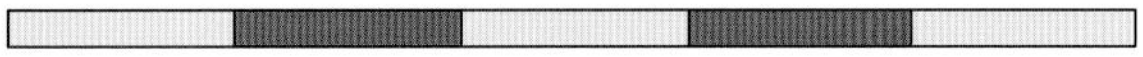

2. Sew 1 square (**O**) to each end of Inner Border to make **Top/Bottom Inner Border**. Make 2 Top/Bottom Inner Borders.

Top/Bottom Inner Border (make 2)

3. Sew 1 **Inner Border** to opposite sides of Quilt Top Center.
4. Sew **Top/Bottom Inner Border** to quilt top.

Outer Border

1. Sew border strips (**E**) together end to end to make 1 outer border strip.
2. To determine length of outer side borders, measure **length** of quilt top. From long outer border strip, cut 2 **outer side borders** the determined length. Matching centers and corners, sew outer side borders to quilt top.
3. To determine length of outer top/bottom borders, measure **width** of quilt top (including added borders). From remaining long outer border strip, cut 2 **outer top/bottom borders** the determined length. Matching centers and corners, sew outer top/bottom borders to quilt top to complete quilt top.

COMPLETING THE QUILT

1. Follow **Quilting**, page 35, to mark, layer, and quilt as desired. Our quilt was machine quilted with a meandering swirl pattern.
2. Refer to **Making a Hanging Sleeve**, page 38, to make and attach a hanging sleeve, if desired.
3. Follow **Binding**, page 39, to bind quilt using binding strips.

Quilt Top Diagram

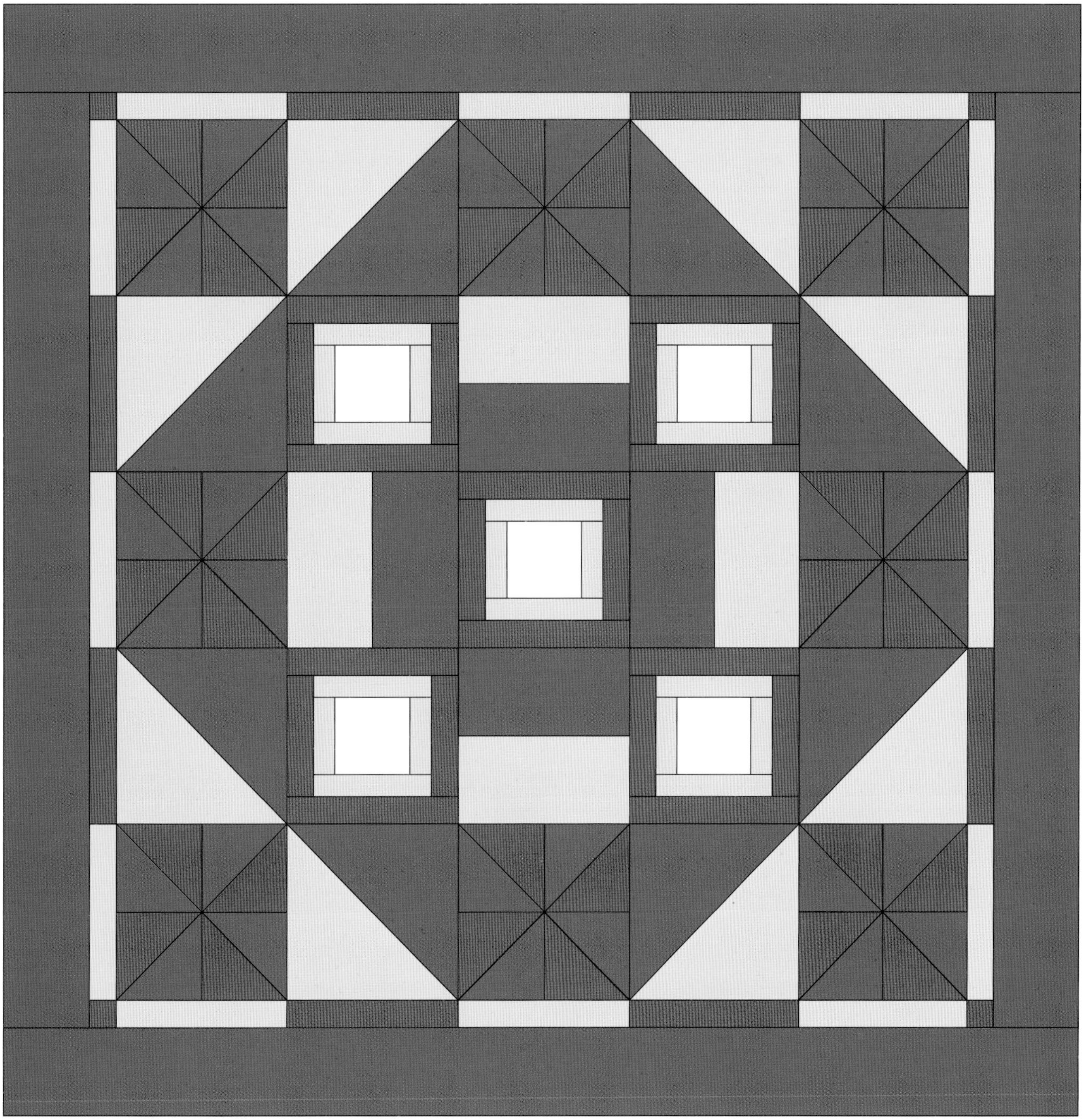

General Instructions

To make your quilting easier and more enjoyable, we encourage you to carefully read all of the general instructions, study the color photographs, and familiarize yourself with the individual project instructions before beginning a project.

FABRICS

SELECTING FABRICS

Choose high-quality, medium-weight 100% cotton fabrics. All-cotton fabrics hold a crease better, fray less, and are easier to quilt than cotton/polyester blends.

Yardage requirements listed for each project are based on 43"/44" wide fabric with a "usable" width of 40" after shrinkage and trimming selvages. Actual usable width will probably vary slightly from fabric to fabric. Our recommended yardage lengths should be adequate for occasional re-squaring of fabric when many cuts are required.

PREPARING FABRICS

We recommend that all fabrics be washed, dried, and pressed before cutting. If fabrics are not pre-washed, washing the finished quilt will cause shrinkage and give it a more "antiqued" look and feel. Bright and dark colors, which may run, should always be washed before cutting. After washing and drying fabric, fold lengthwise with wrong sides together and matching selvages.

ROTARY CUTTING

Rotary cutting has brought speed and accuracy to quiltmaking by allowing quilters to easily cut strips of fabric and then cut those strips into smaller pieces.

- Place fabric on work surface with fold closest to you.
- Cut all strips from the selvage-to-selvage width of the fabric unless otherwise indicated in project instructions.
- Square left edge of fabric using rotary cutter and rulers (**Figs. 1 - 2**).

Fig. 1

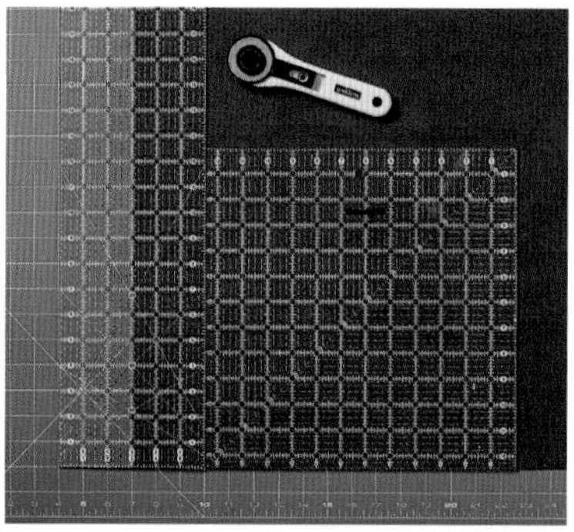

Fig. 2

- To cut each strip required for a project, place ruler over cut edge of fabric, aligning desired marking on ruler with cut edge; make cut (**Fig. 3**).

Fig. 3

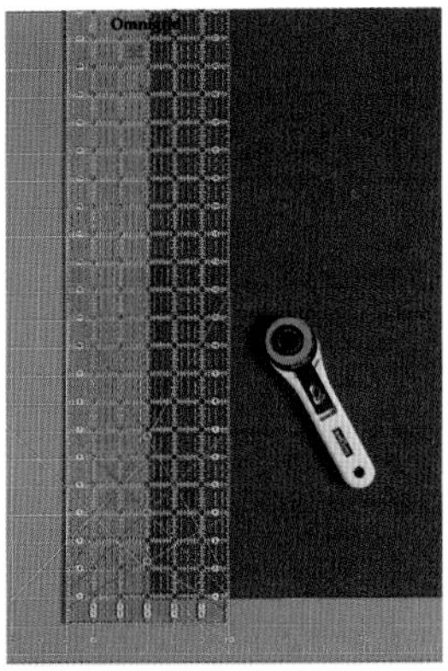

- When cutting several strips from a single piece of fabric, it is important to make sure that cuts remain at a perfect right angle to the fold; square fabric as needed.

MACHINE PIECING

Precise cutting, followed by accurate piecing, will ensure that all pieces of quilt top fit together well.

- Set sewing machine stitch length for approximately 11 stitches per inch.

- Use neutral-colored general-purpose sewing thread (not quilting thread) in needle and in bobbin.

- An accurate 1/4" seam allowance is essential. Presser feet that are 1/4" wide are available for most sewing machines.

- When piecing, always place pieces right sides together and match raw edges; pin if necessary.

- Chain piecing saves time and will usually result in more accurate piecing.

- Trim away points of seam allowances that extend beyond edges of sewn pieces.

SEWING STRIP SETS

When there are several strips to assemble into a strip set, first sew strips together into pairs, then sew pairs together to form strip set. To help avoid distortion, sew seams in opposite directions (**Fig. 4**).

Fig. 4

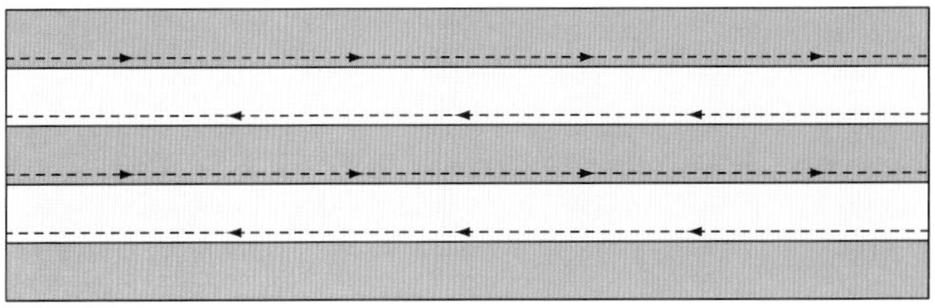

SEWING ACROSS SEAM INTERSECTIONS

When sewing across intersection of two seams, place pieces right sides together and match seams exactly, making sure seam allowances are pressed in opposite directions (**Fig. 5**).

Fig. 5

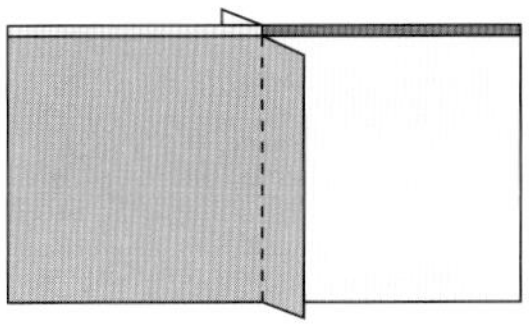

SEWING SHARP POINTS

To ensure sharp points when joining triangular or diagonal pieces, stitch across the center of the "X" (shown in pink) formed on wrong side by previous seams (**Fig. 6**).

Fig. 6

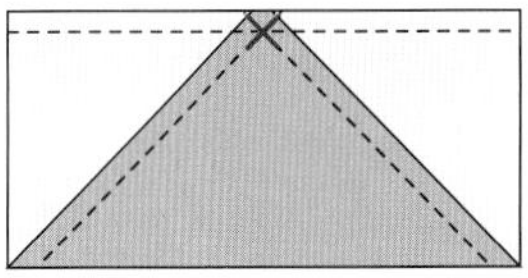

PRESSING

- Use steam iron set on "Cotton" for all pressing.
- Press after sewing each seam.
- Seam allowances are almost always pressed to one side, usually toward darker fabric. However, to reduce bulk it may occasionally be necessary to press seam allowances toward the lighter fabric or even to press them open.
- To prevent dark fabric seam allowance from showing through light fabric, trim darker seam allowance slightly narrower than lighter seam allowance.
- To press long seams, such as those in long strip sets, without curving or other distortion, lay strips across width of the ironing board.

APPLIQUÉ

PREPARING FUSIBLE APPLIQUÉS

White or light-colored fabrics may need to be lined with fusible interfacing before applying fusible web to prevent darker fabrics from showing through.

1. When using fusible web, appliqué patterns need to be reversed from the way they appear on the finished project. To reverse pattern, trace onto tracing paper and turn paper over.
2. Place paper-backed fusible web, paper side up, over appliqué pattern. Trace pattern onto paper side of web with pencil as many times as indicated in project instructions for a single fabric.

3. Follow manufacturer's instructions to fuse traced patterns to wrong side of fabrics. Do not remove paper backing.
4. Use scissors to cut out appliqué pieces along traced lines. Before removing paper backing, lightly mark all embroidery detail lines, if any, on fabric side of appliqué pieces with pencil. Remove paper backing from all pieces. Fuse appliqué pieces in place.

SATIN STITCH APPLIQUÉ

Our satin stitch appliqué features zigzag stitching with a medium stitch length to cover the exposed raw edges of appliqué pieces.

1. Pin stabilizer, such as paper or any of the commercially available products, on wrong side of background fabric before stitching appliqués in place.
2. Thread sewing machine with general-purpose thread; use general-purpose thread that matches background fabric in bobbin.
3. Set sewing machine for a medium (approximately 1/8") zigzag stitch and a medium stitch length. Slightly loosening the top tension may yield a smoother stitch.
4. Begin by stitching two or three stitches in place (drop feed dogs or set stitch length at 0) to anchor thread. Most of the Satin Stitch should be on the appliqué with the right edge of the stitch falling at the outside edge of the appliqué. Stitch over all exposed raw edges of appliqué pieces.
5. (***Note:*** Dots on **Figs. 7 – 12** indicate where to leave needle in fabric when pivoting.) For outside corners, stitch just past corner, stopping with needle in background fabric (**Fig. 7**). Raise presser foot. Pivot project, lower presser foot, and stitch adjacent side (**Fig. 8**).

Fig. 7

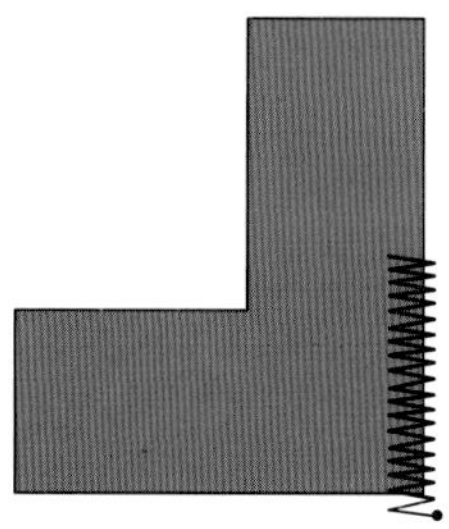

Fig. 8

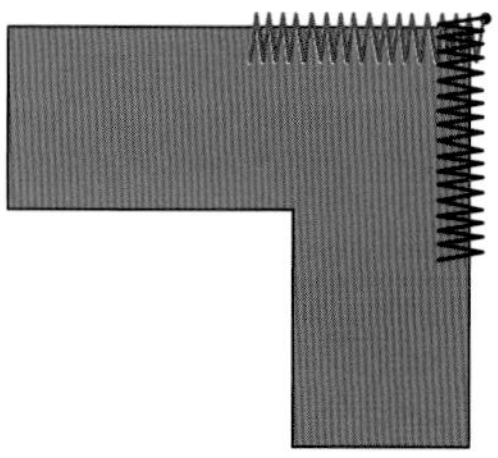

6. For inside corners, stitch just past corner, stopping with needle in appliqué fabric (**Fig. 9**). Raise presser foot. Pivot project, lower presser foot, and stitch adjacent side (**Fig. 10**).

Fig. 9

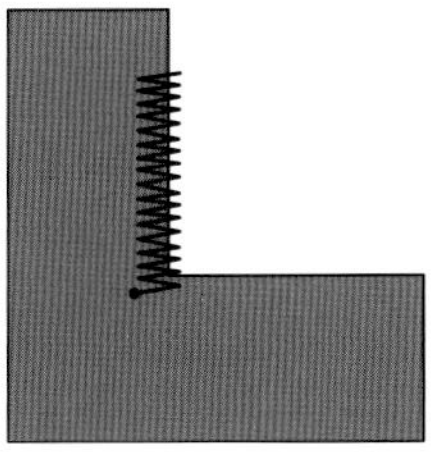

Fig. 10

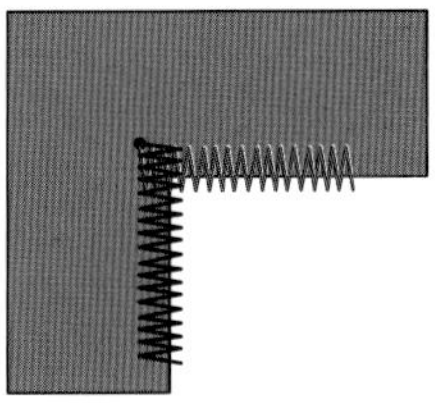

7. When stitching outside curves, stop with needle in background fabric. Raise presser foot and pivot project as needed. Lower presser foot and continue stitching, pivoting as often as necessary to follow curve (**Fig. 11**).

Fig. 11

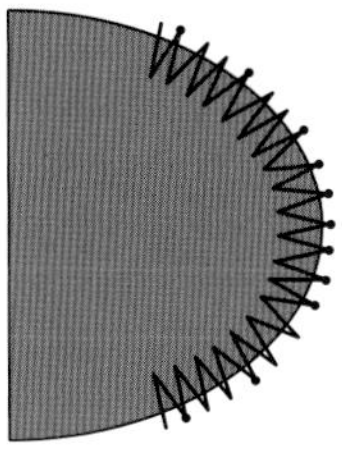

8. When stitching inside curves, stop with needle in appliqué fabric. Raise presser foot and pivot project as needed. Lower presser foot and continue stitching, pivoting as often as necessary to follow curve (**Fig. 12**).

Fig. 12

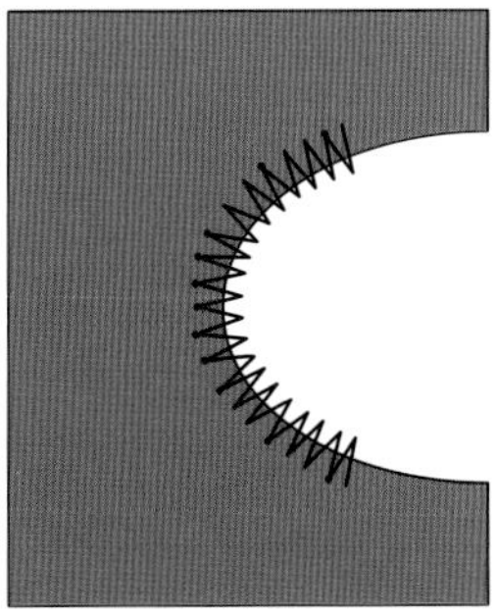

9. Do not backstitch at end of stitching. Pull threads to wrong side of background fabric; knot thread and trim ends.
10. Carefully tear away stabilizer.

QUILTING

*Quilting holds the three layers (top, batting, and backing) of the quilt together and can be done by hand or machine. Because marking, layering, and quilting are interrelated and may be done in different orders depending on circumstances, please read entire **Quilting** section, pages 35 – 38, before beginning project.*

TYPES OF QUILTING DESIGNS

In the Ditch Quilting

Quilting along seamlines or along edges of appliquéd pieces is called "in the ditch" quilting. This type of quilting should be done on side opposite seam allowance and does not have to be marked.

Outline Quilting

Quilting a consistent distance, usually 1/4", from seam or appliqué is called "outline" quilting. Outline quilting may be marked, or 1/4" masking tape may be placed along seamlines for quilting guide. (Do not leave tape on quilt longer than necessary, since it may leave an adhesive residue.)

Motif Quilting

Quilting a design, such as a feathered wreath, is called "motif" quilting. This type of quilting should be marked before basting quilt layers together.

Echo Quilting

Quilting that follows the outline of an appliquéd or pieced design with two or more parallel lines is called "echo" quilting. This type of quilting does not need to be marked.

Channel Quilting

Quilting with straight, parallel lines is called "channel" quilting. This type of quilting may be marked or stitched using a guide.

Crosshatch Quilting

Quilting straight lines in a grid pattern is called "crosshatch" quilting. Lines may be stitched parallel to edges of quilt or stitched diagonally. This type of quilting may be marked or stitched using a guide.

Meandering Quilting

Quilting in random curved lines and swirls is called "meandering" quilting. Quilting lines should not cross or touch each other. This type of quilting does not need to be marked.

Stipple Quilting

Meandering quilting that is very closely spaced is called "stipple" quilting. Stippling will flatten the area quilted and is often stitched in background areas to raise appliquéd or pieced designs. This type of quilting does not need to be marked.

MARKING QUILTING LINES

Quilting lines may be marked using fabric marking pencils, chalk markers, water- or air-soluble pens, or lead pencils.

Simple quilting designs may be marked with chalk or chalk pencil after basting. A small area may be marked, then quilted, before moving to next area to be marked. Intricate designs should be marked before basting using a more durable marker.

Caution: Pressing may permanently set some marks. Test different markers on scrap fabric to find one that marks clearly and can be thoroughly removed.

A wide variety of pre-cut quilting stencils, as well as entire books of quilting patterns, are available. Using a stencil makes it easier to mark intricate or repetitive designs.

To make a stencil from a pattern, center template plastic over pattern and use a permanent marker to trace pattern onto plastic. Use a craft knife with single or double blade to cut channels along traced lines (**Fig. 13**).

Fig. 13

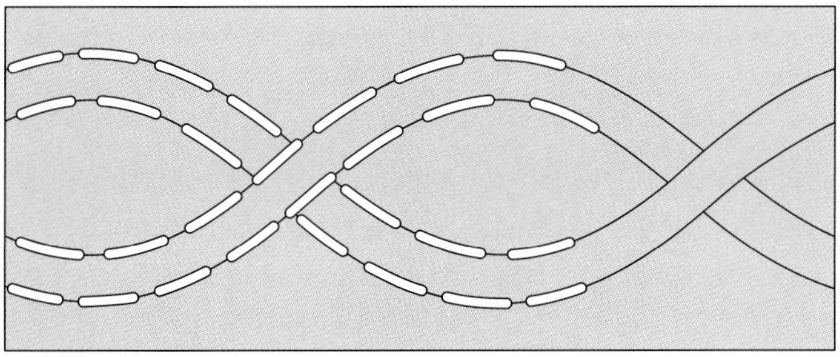

PREPARING THE BACKING

To allow for slight shifting of quilt top during quilting, backing should be approximately 4" larger on all sides. Yardage requirements listed for quilt backings are calculated for 43"/44"w fabric. Using 90"w or 108"w fabric for the backing of a bed-sized quilt may eliminate piecing. To piece a backing using 43"/44"w fabric, use the following instructions.

1. Measure length and width of quilt top; add 8" to each measurement.
2. Cut backing fabric into two lengths the determined *length* measurement. Trim selvages. Place lengths with right sides facing and sew long edges together, forming tube (**Fig. 14**). Match seams and press along one fold (**Fig. 15**). Cut along pressed fold to form single piece (**Fig. 16**).

Fig. 14

Fig. 15

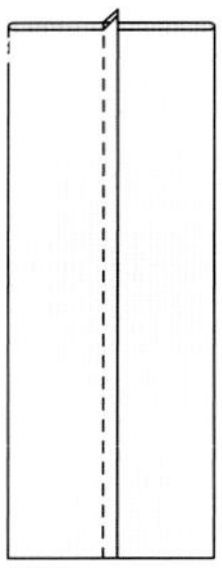

Fig. 16

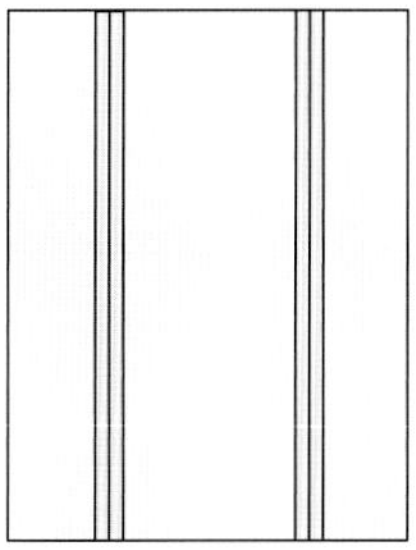

3. Trim backing to size determined in Step 1; press seam allowances open.

CHOOSING THE BATTING

The appropriate batting will make quilting easier. For fine hand quilting, choose low-loft batting. All cotton or cotton/polyester blend battings work well for machine quilting because the cotton helps "grip" quilt layers. If quilt is to be tied, a high-loft batting, sometimes called extra-loft or fat batting, may be used to make quilt "fluffy."

Types of batting include cotton, polyester, wool, silk, cotton/polyester blend, and cotton/wool blend.

When selecting batting, refer to package labels for characteristics and care instructions. Cut batting same size as prepared backing.

ASSEMBLING THE QUILT

1. Examine wrong side of quilt top closely; trim any seam allowances and clip any threads that may show through front of the quilt. Press quilt top, being careful not to "set" any marked quilting lines.
2. Place backing wrong side up on flat surface. Use masking tape to tape edges of backing to surface. Place batting on top of backing fabric. Smooth batting gently, being careful not to stretch or tear. Center quilt top right side up on batting.
3. Use 1" rustproof safety pins to "pin-baste" all layers together, spacing pins approximately 4" apart. Begin at center and work toward outer edges to secure all layers. If possible, place pins away from areas that will be quilted, although pins may be removed as needed when quilting.

MACHINE QUILTING METHODS

Use general-purpose thread in bobbin. Do not use quilting thread. Thread the needle of machine with general-purpose thread or transparent monofilament thread to make quilting blend with quilt top fabrics. Use decorative thread, such as a metallic or contrasting-color general-purpose thread, to make quilting lines stand out more.

Straight-Line Quilting

The term "straight-line" is somewhat deceptive, since curves (especially gentle ones) as well as straight lines can be stitched with this technique.

1. Set stitch length for six to ten stitches per inch and attach walking foot to sewing machine.
2. Determine which section of quilt will have longest continuous quilting line, oftentimes area from center top to center bottom. Roll up and secure each edge of quilt to help reduce the bulk, keeping fabrics smooth. Smaller projects may not need to be rolled.
3. Begin stitching on longest quilting line, using very short stitches for the first 1/4" to "lock" quilting. Stitch across project, using one hand on each side of walking foot to slightly spread fabric and to guide fabric through machine. Lock stitches at end of quilting line.
4. Continue machine quilting, stitching longer quilting lines first to stabilize quilt before moving on to other areas.

Free-Motion Quilting

Free-motion quilting may be free form or may follow a marked pattern.

1. Attach darning foot to sewing machine and lower or cover feed dogs.
2. Position quilt under darning foot; lower foot. Holding top thread, take a stitch and pull bobbin thread to top of quilt. To "lock" beginning of quilting line, hold top and bobbin threads while making three to five stitches in place.
3. Use one hand on each side of darning foot to slightly spread fabric and to move fabric through the machine. Even stitch length is achieved by using smooth, flowing hand motion and steady machine speed. Slow machine speed and fast hand movement will create long stitches. Fast machine speed and slow hand movement will create short stitches. Move quilt sideways, back and forth, in a circular motion, or in a random motion to create desired designs; do not rotate quilt. Lock stitches at end of each quilting line.

MAKING A HANGING SLEEVE

Attaching a hanging sleeve to back of wall hanging or quilt before the binding is added allows project to be displayed on wall.

1. Measure width of quilt top edge and subtract 1". Cut piece of fabric 7"w by determined measurement.
2. Press short edges of fabric piece 1/4" to wrong side; press edges 1/4" to wrong side again and machine stitch in place.
3. Matching wrong sides, fold piece in half lengthwise to form tube.
4. Follow project instructions to sew binding to quilt top and to trim backing and batting. Before Blindstitching binding to backing, match raw edges and stitch hanging sleeve to center top edge on back of quilt.
5. Finish binding quilt, treating hanging sleeve as part of backing.
6. Blindstitch bottom of hanging sleeve to backing, taking care not to stitch through to front of quilt.
7. Insert dowel or slat into hanging sleeve.

BINDING

1. Using a diagonal seam (**Fig. 17**), sew binding strips together end to end.

Fig. 17

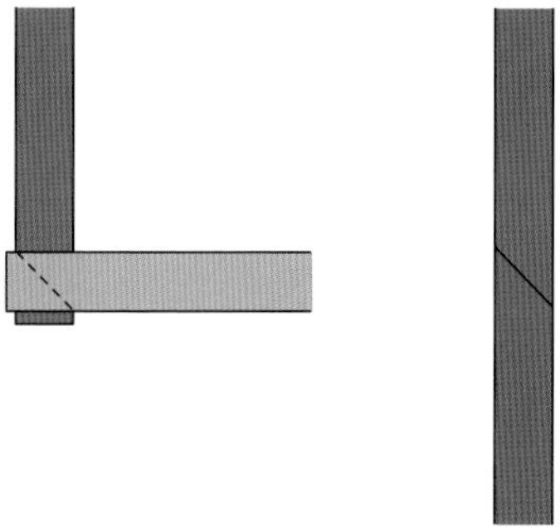

2. Matching wrong sides and raw edges, press binding strips in half lengthwise.
3. Beginning with one end near center on bottom edge of quilt, lay binding around quilt to make sure that seams in binding will not end up at a corner. Adjust placement if necessary. Matching raw edges of binding to raw edge of quilt top, pin binding to right side of quilt along one edge.
4. When you reach first corner, mark 1/4" from corner of quilt top (**Fig. 18**).

Fig. 18

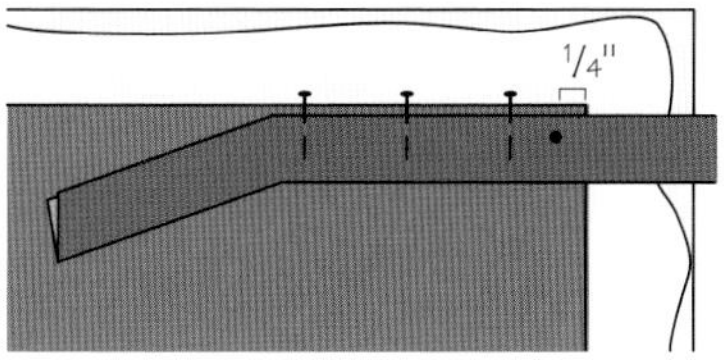

5. Beginning approximately 10" from end of binding and using 1/4" seam allowance, sew binding to quilt, backstitching at beginning of stitching and at mark (**Fig. 19**). Lift needle out of fabric and clip thread.

Fig. 19

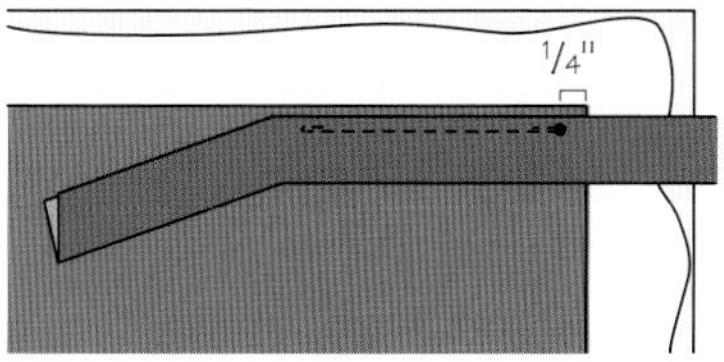

6. Fold binding as shown in **Figs. 20 – 21** and pin binding to adjacent side, matching raw edges. When you've reached the next corner, mark 1/4" from edge of quilt top.

Fig. 20

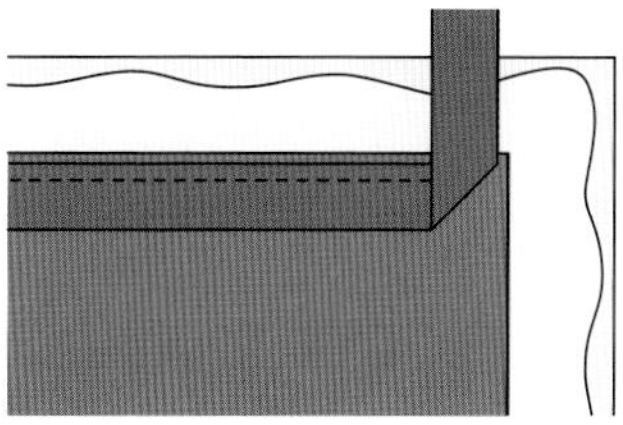

Fig. 21

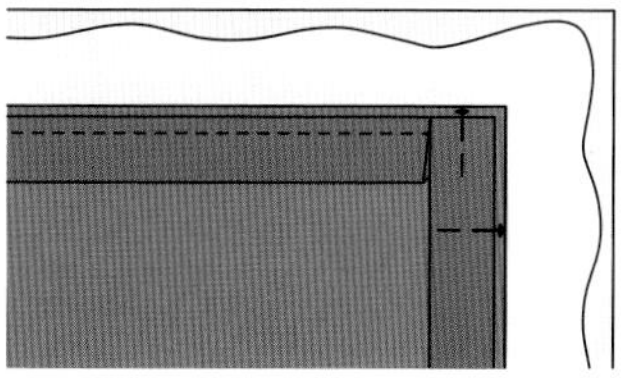

7. Backstitching at edge of quilt top, sew pinned binding to quilt (**Fig. 22**); backstitch at the next mark. Lift needle out of fabric and clip thread.

Fig. 22

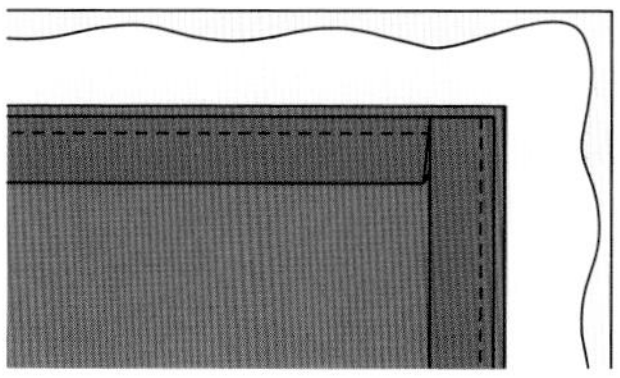

8. Continue sewing binding to quilt, stopping approximately 10" from starting point (**Fig. 23**).

Fig. 23

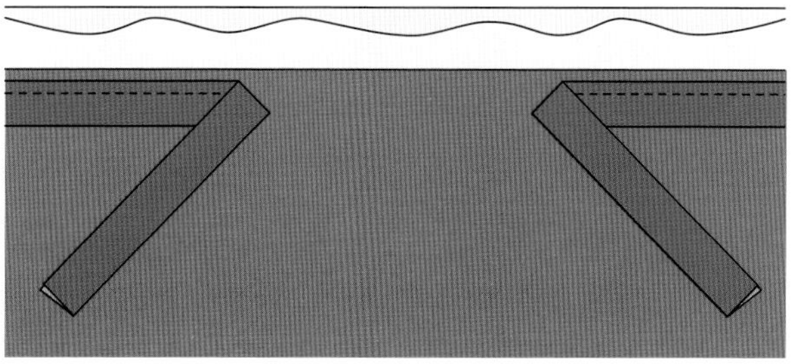

9. Bring beginning and end of binding to center of opening and fold each end back, leaving a 1/4" space between folds (**Fig. 24**). Finger press folds.

Fig. 24

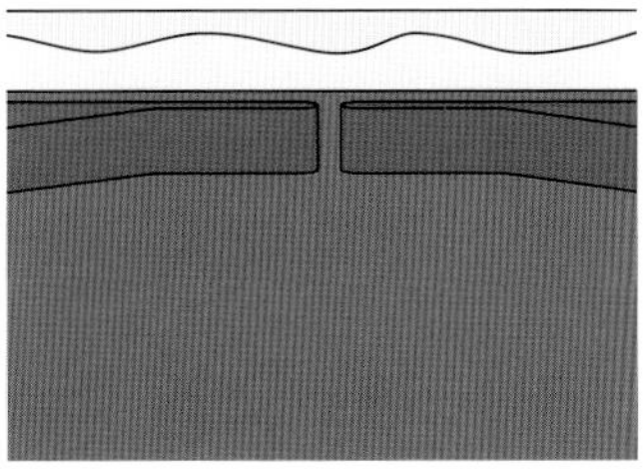

10. Unfold ends of binding and draw a line across wrong side in finger-pressed crease. Draw a line through the lengthwise pressed fold of binding at the same spot to create a cross mark. With edge of ruler at cross mark, line up 45° angle marking on ruler with one long side of binding. Draw a diagonal line from edge to edge. Repeat on remaining end, making sure that the two diagonal lines are angled the same way (**Fig. 25**).

Fig. 25

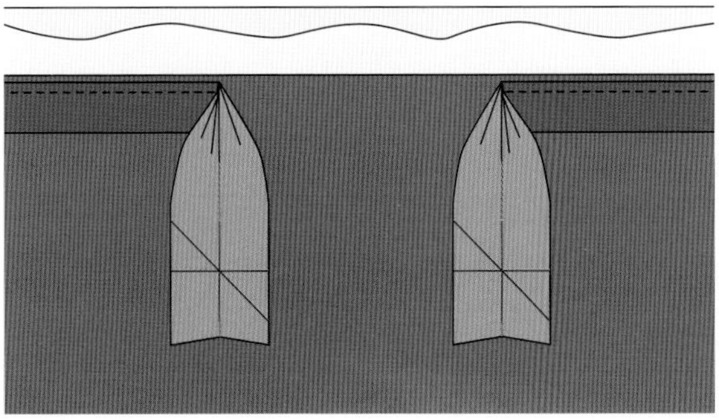

11. Matching right sides and diagonal lines, pin binding ends together a right angles (**Fig. 26**).

Fig. 26

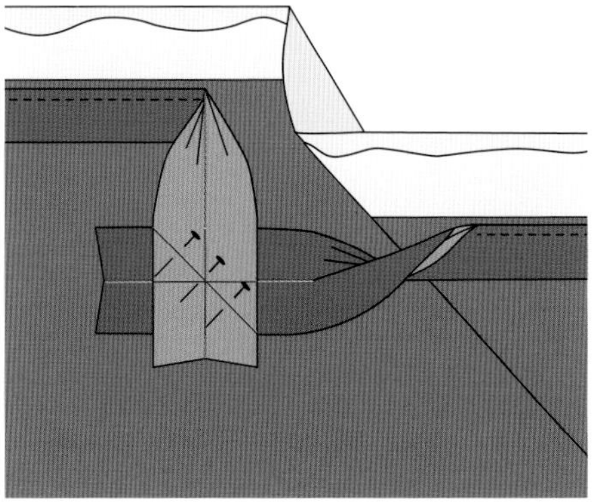

12. Machine stitch along diagonal line (**Fig. 27**), removing pins as you stitch.

Fig. 27

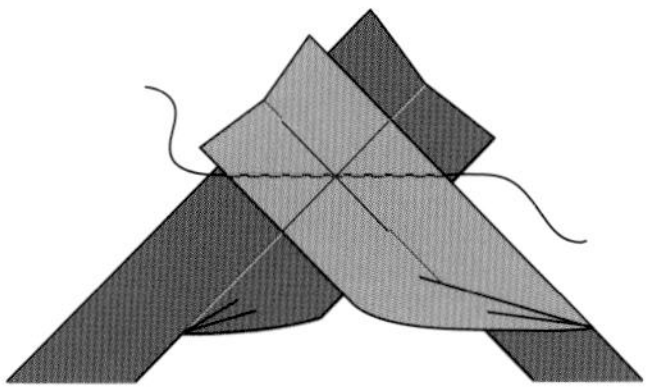

13. Lay binding against quilt to double check that it is correct length.
14. Trim binding ends, leaving 1/4" seam allowance; press seam open. Stitch binding to quilt.
15. Trim backing and batting even with edges of quilt top.

16. On one edge of quilt, fold binding over to quilt backing and pin pressed edge in place, covering stitching line (**Fig. 28**). On adjacent side, fold binding over, forming a mitered corner (**Fig. 29**). Repeat to pin remainder of binding in place.

Fig. 28

Fig. 29

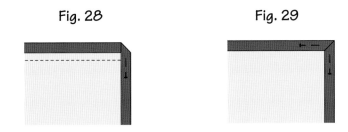

17. Blindstitch (page 42) binding to backing, taking care not to stitch through to front of quilt.

SIGNING AND DATING YOUR QUILT

A completed quilt is a work of art and should be signed and dated. There are many different ways to do this and numerous books on the subject. The label should reflect the style of the quilt, the occasion or person for which it was made, and the quilter's own particular talents. Following are suggestions for recording the history of quilt or adding a sentiment for future generations.

- Embroider quilter's name, date, and any additional information on quilt top or backing. Matching floss, such as cream floss on white border, will leave a subtle record. Bright or contrasting floss will make the information stand out.
- Make label from muslin and use permanent marker to write information. Use different colored permanent markers to make label more decorative. Stitch label to back of quilt.
- Use photo-transfer paper to add image to white or cream fabric label. Stitch label to back of quilt.
- Piece an extra block from quilt top pattern to use as label. Add information with permanent fabric pen. Appliqué block to back of quilt.
- Write message on appliquéd design from quilt top. Attach appliqué to back of the quilt.

Hand Stitches

BLANKET STITCH

Come up at 1, go down at 2, and come up at 3, keeping thread below point of needle (**Fig. 30**).

Fig. 30

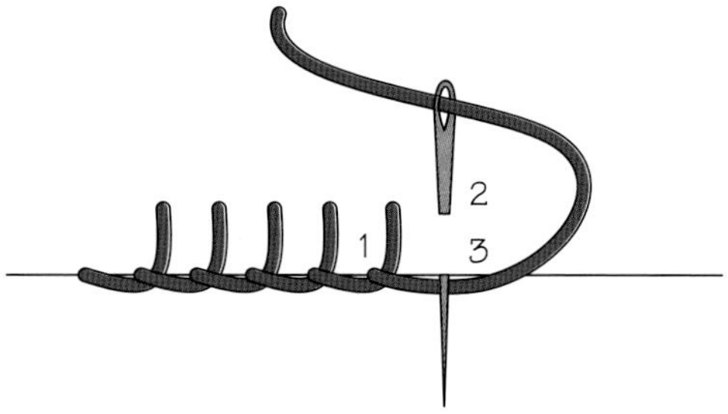

BLINDSTITCH

A Blindstitch should be almost invisible from the right side of the fabrics. Come up at 1, go down at 2, and come up at 3 (**Fig. 31**).

Fig. 31

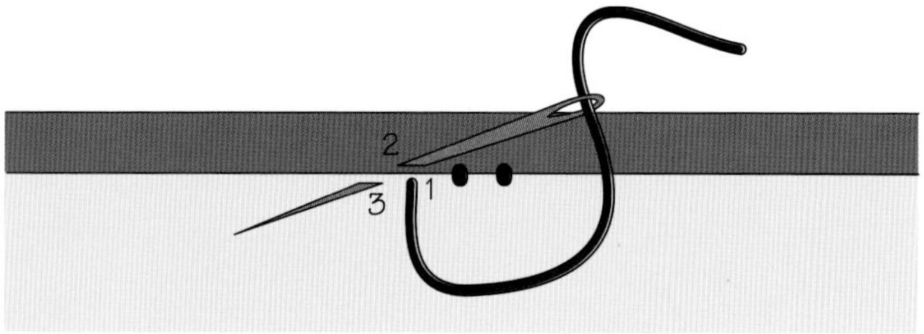

FRENCH KNOT

Follow **Fig. 32** to complete French Knot. Come up at 1. Wrap thread once around needle and insert needle at 2, holding end of thread with non-stitching fingers. Tighten knot, then pull needle through, holding floss until it must be released.

Fig. 32

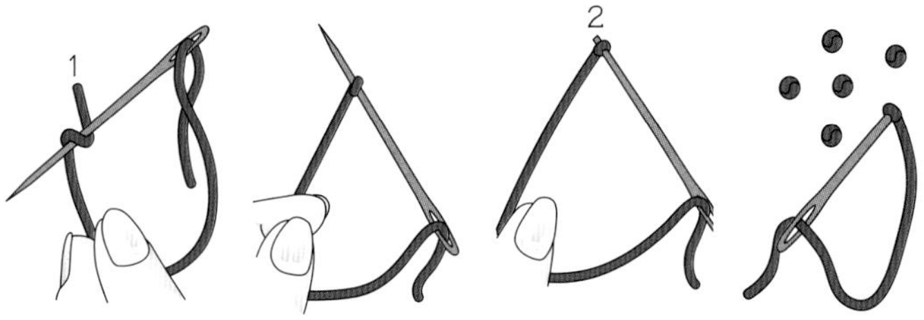

SATIN STITCH

Come up at 1, go down at 2, and come up at 3. Continue until area is filled (**Fig. 33**). Work stitches close together, but not overlapping.

Fig. 33

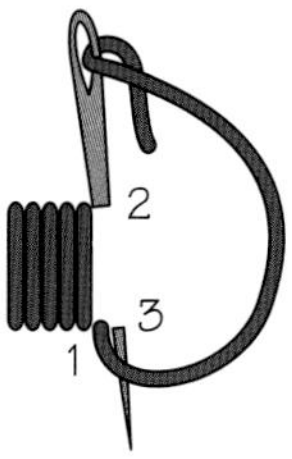

STEM STITCH

Come up at 1. Keeping thread below the stitching line, go down at 2 and come up at 3. Go down at 4 and come up at 5 (**Fig. 34**).

Fig. 34

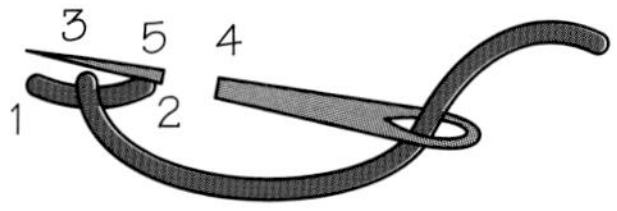

Metric Conversion Chart

Inches x 2.54 = centimeters (cm)	Yards x .9144 = meters (m)
Inches x 25.4 = millimeters (mm)	Yards x 91.44 = centimeters (cm)
Inches x .0254 = meters (m)	Centimeters x .3937 = inches (")
	Meters x 1.0936 = yards (yd)

Standard Equivalents

1/8"	3.2 mm	0.32 cm	1/8 yard	11.43 cm	0.11 m
1/4"	6.35 mm	0.635 cm	1/4 yard	22.86 cm	0.23 m
3/8"	9.5 mm	0.95 cm	3/8 yard	34.29 cm	0.34 m
1/2"	12.7 mm	1.27 cm	1/2 yard	45.72 cm	0.46 m
5/8"	15.9 mm	1.59 cm	5/8 yard	57.15 cm	0.57 m
3/4"	19.1 mm	1.91 cm	3/4 yard	68.58 cm	0.69 m
7/8"	22.2 mm	2.22 cm	7/8 yard	80 cm	0.8 m
1"	25.4 mm	2.54 cm	1 yard	91.44 cm	0.91 m

meet the Designers....

Cotton Pickin' Designs is the creative artistry of Debbie Foley and Valerie Boman. Debbie and Valerie first met while teaching at a quilt store in Phoenix. Each had tried her hand at designing before, and the two agreed to collaborate on a "block of the month" for the shop.

While working together, Debbie and Valerie quickly discovered the similarity in their ideas. They continued designing and teaching collectively for three more years, until local quilters finally convinced them to start a pattern business.

The resulting company, Cotton Pickin' Designs, is committed to offering quilters a wide variety of colorful, exciting designs featuring a profusion of fabrics.

Visit www.cottonpickindesigns.com to see more of Debbie and Valerie's quilt patterns, or check your local retailer or www.leisurearts.com to find more Leisure Arts leaflets by Cotton Pickin' Designs.

The inspiration for these cute quilts—
Valerie's grandchildren, Mitchel & Cameron.

Production Team:

Technical Writer
Lisa Lancaster

Editorial Writer
Susan McManus Johnson

Graphic Designer
Amy Gerke

Graphic Artist
Frances Huddleston

Photography Stylist
Angela Alexander

We have made every effort to ensure that these instructions are accurate and complete. We cannot, however, be responsible for human error, typographical mistakes, or variations in individual work.